THE CHANGING GAME

MARTIN O'NEILL
THE CHANGING GAME

The past, present and future of football

With Joey D'Urso

WELBECK

First published in 2025 by Headline Welbeck Non-Fiction
An imprint of Headline Publishing Group Limited

1

Cataloguing in Publication Data is available from the British Library

Hardback ISBN 978 1 0354 2999 8
Trade Paperback ISBN 978 1 0354 3000 0

Typeset in Warnock Pro by CC Book Production

Printed and bound in Great Britain by Clays Ltd, Elcograf S.p.A.

Headline Publishing Group Limited
An Hachette UK Company
Carmelite House
50 Victoria Embankment
London EC4Y 0DZ

The authorised representative in the EEA is Hachette Ireland,
8 Castlecourt Centre, Dublin 15, D15 XTP3, Ireland
(email: info@hbgi.ie)

www.headline.co.uk
www.hachette.co.uk

To Caragh Gene and Loulia

CONTENTS

THE CHANGING GAME

INTRODUCTION

The End at Nottingham Forest

A bright Friday afternoon sun is breaking through some billowy clouds hanging over the fine city of Nottingham, affording much needed warmth to the end of the month. It is the last Friday in June 2019. Office workers, hoping to grab some extra hours for the weekend ahead, are making their way home, crossing the famous Trent Bridge on foot, and by car or bus. Any commuter stealing a glance to the left cannot miss the football stadium, rising majestically, it seems, from the fast-flowing river below. Home to Nottingham Forest Football Club, the arena has witnessed some incredible scenes in its proud history. Those of an older generation swear the tumult caused some sort of earthquake when the magnificent goalscoring winger Ian Storey-Moore headed the winning goal against Everton in a pulsating FA Cup quarter-final tie inside those hallowed walls back in 1967. And if that wasn't enough, along came the charismatic Brian Clough less than a decade later to weave his magic and turn the football club into champions of

Europe. Yes, champions of Europe, not once, but twice over. The latter day Robin Hood was a demigod. Letters flowed into his office demanding that he walk on the River Trent rather than take one of the kayaks belonging to the nearby rowing club along the riverbank. Those were heady days indeed, and I was privileged to be part of that unparalleled run of success under the leadership of a footballing genius. But today, Friday 28 June 2019, those moments are well and truly confined to history and now the club finds itself in the second tier of English football, having been peering up at the Premier League's riches for 20 years.

I am the manager of the club. I had signed an 18-month contract in January with one aim in mind: promotion to the Promised Land. I have overseen the last 19 games of the previous season and am looking forward to the months ahead. The owner, Evangelos Marinakis, told me in January that he would bring in new players to augment a squad essentially short of real quality, saying a concerted effort to win promotion would begin this pre-season. It was music to my ears when I signed.

At this very moment I am sitting with my coaching staff having a bite of lunch in the Robin Hood suite, perched within the club's grounds. Out of the corner of my eye I catch a glimpse of Kyriakos Dourekas, or Koulis, the director of football, coming towards our table, not looking too pleased with life. A few weeks earlier he and I were in Athens together, where I learned, though not from him, that he had been a swimming instructor in an earlier life before he met Mr Marinakis. He tells me now that the chief executive wants to see me in the directors' suite immediately. I don't like his tone so I answer that I will finish my lunch first before I see anyone. He turns and stomps off. I look over to my goalkeeping coach, Seamus McDonagh. He looks concerned. So does Steve Guppy, my first-team coach. If truth be told, I'm probably a little anxious myself.

I walk into the directors' suite about five minutes later, a room I know so very well. It was here that Brian Clough and Peter Taylor used to vent their spleens at my expense all those years ago – it's not necessarily my favourite room. There are three people there, waiting for my arrival. Koulis and chief executive Ioannis Vrentzos have been joined by another man, an ex-professional French footballer who is the chief scout of Olympiacos, the owner's other club, in Greece. He has been around since January, ostensibly to help with recruitment of players, but little has happened on that front. Ioannis takes the lead. He tells me that the way I am running the football club is not the way they want the club to be run. I could tell them, if they wanted to listen, that, actually, I have won the last three league games we have played, but that was all of 54 days ago so I don't expect them to remember. In fact, I hardly remember myself. However, I am disappointed and narked.

Ioannis wants to explain the decision to sack me, or at least I think he does, but I don't want to hear what he has to say. It is no surprise to me that he had been lining up someone else. My annoyance is that the owner had summoned me to see him in Greece just two weeks beforehand, and he had been as nice as could be. I did sense something was up upon returning and seeing that a couple of the things I'd asked for – sorting out the pitch, for one – had not been done. So this was it. I did not want to hear any more. Nothing will change anyway. I turn and walk away. I have been in the directors' suite for close on 100 seconds. As I walk out the door I cannot help but glance to my left. A few yards away lies the manager's office, ironically not in use these days. Great managers of the past have housed themselves in that very room. The legendary Dave Mackay brought me into his headquarters to tell me that I was a really good footballer, and coming from him that was praise indeed. He was only manager here for 12 months but made such an impression on me that if I wanted to be anybody else in another life, I would want to be Dave Mackay. Then there was Matt Gillies, the Scottish gentleman who signed me in October 1971 thus allowing me to live the dream of being a professional footballer. And, of course, the immortal Brian Clough who, from that very room, plotted the historic course of this club.

I reach my own office and summon Seamus and Steve to tell them that we are no longer in employment at Nottingham Forest. They are genuinely taken aback, despite seeing Koulis's sour face ten minutes earlier. We sit down, take some tea and ruminate. Suddenly Seamus's phone rings. It's his daughter Amy, telling him that Nottingham Forest have appointed a new manager and a full complement of coaching staff. We haven't even left the building. Twenty-four minutes have elapsed since I left the directors' suite. I completely understand that's the business of football, but 24 minutes may well be a record from sacking one manager to the appointment of another. Then again . . . maybe not?

The new manager, Sabri Lamouchi, signs about 15 players in the next few weeks and makes a real fist of promotion, just failing to make the play-offs. And some of those nondescript players fall by the wayside, no doubt complaining to Koulis and Ioannis that the manager hasn't treated them with the respect they deserve. Honours have eluded them, but it has never been their fault. Regardless, the irony is not lost on me. I came into the professional game almost 50 years ago, through a door at the City Ground, Nottingham. I leave the professional game through the very same door. And I wonder what those 50 years are all about.

The Beginning at Nottingham Forest

Football, as one might imagine, would have made significant strides to keep pace with an ever-changing world. In October 1971, I leave a trouble-torn Northern Ireland, in political upheaval for a long time before, but now about two years into a 30-year struggle forever to be known as 'The Troubles'. A new life awaits me over the Irish Sea. I am England-bound, heading to Nottingham to start a life as a professional footballer.

INTRODUCTION

The previous 12 months, since I first joined an Irish league team called Distillery, has been an accelerated rise to prominence for me in Northern Irish football. Two goals in the final of the Irish Cup against Derby City in April of this very year sealing not only victory on the day but a place in the upcoming European Cup Winners' Cup. Barcelona, drawn out of the hat, are our illustrious opponents. A goal against them in Belfast followed by a strong individual performance in the Nou Camp gives me much traction, both locally and nationally, causing a few English clubs to take notice. A few weeks later, the withdrawal of some players through injury from the senior international team to play Russia allows the manager, Terry Neill, to bring me into the squad. Sharing a dressing room with Pat Jennings, Pat Rice, Sammy Nelson and other top-class footballers is an awesome experience, that is as clear to me now as it was a half century ago.

I get to the field of play against Russia for the last quarter of the game. Those 20-odd minutes are, incredibly, very vague, but the following week is etched in my memory forever. Nottingham Forest post a £15,000 bid to Distillery for me. It is accepted on a Tuesday evening and the following morning I find myself at the gates of the City Ground with one small suitcase in hand and a headful of dreams and aspirations. A new world, seemingly a long distance away from where I had spent the previous 19 years, awaits me. If truth be told I am not really sure what to expect. Reality has never been the same as fantasy land but the excitement of being a professional footballer is intoxicating and

I do not want to spurn this big opportunity. What I experience over the next half century are some incredible moments, both joyous and heartbreaking, perhaps in equal measure.

But while I start this footballing odyssey, my homeland becomes an unsafe place to live. My parents and younger siblings remain in Belfast for a few more months until I sort myself out, get my geographical bearings around Nottingham and find some suitable accommodation for them before they leave Northern Ireland, perhaps forever.

Within a few weeks I force myself into Forest's first team, make my debut as a substitute at the City Ground against West Bromwich Albion, score a blinding half-volley within 15 minutes of coming on to the pitch and celebrate a resounding 4–1 victory with teammates that less than six weeks earlier I had only known through edited *Match of the Day* TV highlights.

At Old Trafford a few weeks later I do the same again, this time within four minutes of entry on to the hallowed turf in the Theatre of Dreams, and with the legendary trio of Best, Law and Charlton on the same field. I pick the ball up inside my own half, burst past a couple of United players and when nearing the edge of their penalty area unleash a drive past Alex Stepney who made that wondrous save from Eusebio in the 1968 European Cup Final at Wembley, thus allowing Manchester United to draw breath once again and go on to beat Benfica in extra-time to become the first English team to win the most coveted trophy in European Football. Am I thinking about all this as the ball hits the back of United's net? Probably not, but the exhilaration I feel right now makes me momentarily sure I have arrived in the big time. After all, Manchester United are today clear leaders in the illustrious league known as the First Division, and George Best, one of the greatest footballers of all time, has just witnessed me scoring this goal against his club from just about 50 yards away. Why shouldn't I believe I have hit the big time? What an easy game this is turning out to be, I think to myself. And what a shock I am going to get for at least another five or six years. However, this late afternoon in the city of Manchester, I am on top of the world.

This book attempts, through my own prism, to view the changes that have taken place in the footballing world over the last 50 years. From that day in December 1971 when Manchester United went from being five points clear at the top of the table – in the day when there were two points for a win – to a meek surrender by the end of that season, and then to unthinkable relegation a few seasons later. When Derby County, under the leadership of a brash, self-important but charismatic young manager called Brian Clough, clinched the title, and in so doing brought both Clough and his assistant manager Peter Taylor into the limelight that they never really left, even in some of their less remarkable moments.

Changes in life are inevitable. So why not football? And I have witnessed many changes in the professional game, some good, some not so good. This is a book about the development of football in the last half century. From aspects like how we deal with injuries, foreign influences on the British game, the changing roles of managers and coaches, players and agents. The effect of social media, wage structures, and a few rule conversions adding to the mix. Of course, frustration with certain aspects of today's game can be utterly riling. Playacting, feigning injury, diving, call it what you will, have reached embarrassing levels. The tenure of a coach at any level is statistically much shorter today than it has ever been, probably thrust forward by the rush to judgement when two or three results go wrong.

My life and career have not been concerned with politics, although it is sometimes hard to avoid it, especially when you are a Catholic Northern Irishman captaining the country's football team (which is mainly supported by Protestants), or managing Celtic, the traditionally Catholic team in Glasgow. My life and career have been in football, lifting the European Cup twice at Nottingham Forest, and managing clubs like Leicester City and Aston Villa in England's Premier League. My football career began in 1971 and ended with that last management job at Nottingham Forest in 2019, although I have continued to be deeply involved in the game since then as a media pundit as well as chair of the League Managers' Association.

I have seen lots of changes, some of them good, some of them perhaps not so good, but I still love the game. It's impossible not to.

There are doubtless many things that are far better now, though. A football ground is a safer place to go. During my career many fans went to a football stadium and never came home, killed in crushes or fires. The game has professionalised, and people take things like diet and injuries more seriously. It is easy to romanticise the game of hard tackles, muddy pitches and shared baths, but modern medicine has prolonged careers that ended far too early when I was a player. The top level of the game is brilliant to watch as well: fast-paced, energetic and exciting. It is a simple game and a magical one and it is a privilege to have spent so long working in it. The game has changed, for sure, and it will change some more in the years to come, but the essence of it remains the same – the importance of team spirit, the way that winning or losing a game changes your entire mood for a week, and the basics of attacking and defending.

When you are a footballer, you are so immersed in the day-to-day of the game that you rarely take in things outside of that little bubble, but one memory sticks out as an example of how the wider world has changed, as well as football. In November 1974 I was firmly established as a top-level footballer and had a free Tuesday evening so chose to travel from Nottingham to the Birmingham Odeon for a concert to see the band Jethro Tull with a teammate. That journey was not as simple as it is now – it was a long drive in my first car, which I had just bought, and we got lost. There was no sat-nav or anything like that, of course. We realised we were very lost and thought we were going to be late for the concert, but somewhere around Lichfield we spotted a girl at a bus stop. I stopped the car and wound down the window and said, 'Excuse me, will you tell me the way into Birmingham city centre?' She said she was heading that way to meet her boyfriend, which was incredible luck, so she jumped into the car and we drove on. Because of her directing us, we went from running late to being early. We said, 'The least we can do is buy you a drink,' so we went to this pub about 200 or 300 yards from the Odeon. We got in, went down the steps, had a drink and said, 'Thank you very much.' We went our separate ways and headed on to the concert. That was a Tuesday night about seven o'clock, and Jethro Tull was one of the first concerts I'd been to. I really enjoyed it.

But had that Jethro Tull concert been on the Thursday rather than the Tuesday, we would have all been blown up, and my professional football life would have ended before it had barely begun, with no European Cups and no career in management. The Tavern in the Town was bombed by the Provisional IRA and 21 people were killed. It was the deadliest act of terrorism on the UK mainland between the Second World War and the London bombings in 2005. When I was manager of Aston Villa many years later – just a couple of miles down the road from the Tavern in the Town – I got the chance to meet the drummer of Jethro Tull, who was a big Villa fan, and spoke to him about that evening, although he didn't remember the ominous timing of that concert all those years ago.

I tell these stories to illustrate the vast changes that have taken place since then, not in some distant place but on the British mainland, where life as a Northern Irishman was often not easy. Those events of the early 1970s seem a world away now. An Irish accent in England in the seventies was often remarked upon, although you sort of had a non-political status as a footballer, certainly when it came to other players. But if you walked in somewhere and nobody knew who you were you could get a hostile reception, people assuming perhaps that I was on the side of those committing such acts. Which, of course, I absolutely wasn't – although I do agree with the republican cause, which is thankfully now being sought through peaceful means. The Catholics in Northern Ireland were having a terrible time in the 1970s, but it is hard to make nuanced arguments when people are being killed.

My football career began five years after England won the World Cup. I was 14 years old in 1966, growing up in Northern Ireland rather than England, but it was a huge thing. England was the home of football, where the game originated, but Brazil were the favourites, having won in 1958 and 1962. England won the final at Wembley and the Football League got a major boost in terms of crowds coming to matches after that. Following the competition from a distance in Northern Ireland, I decided I wanted to become a professional player. And I achieved that goal at the age of 19, as a student at Queen's University, studying law, while playing part-time for Distillery. One Tuesday afternoon I was in the students' union in Belfast, and I heard that Northern Ireland wanted me to play for them. Shortly afterwards, Nottingham Forest had made a bid for me and it was accepted. The next morning I was winging my way to Nottingham.

Nottingham Forest were struggling at the time. The season after the World Cup in 1966 they had finished as runners-up to Manchester United in the league but that team had disintegrated and morale was low. They had a great player in Ian Storey-Moore but were really struggling at the bottom of the league. None of that mattered to me. I probably thought I'd go along and save them, or something. Within a few weeks I got the goal at West Bromwich Albion, and then in December the one at Old Trafford, after coming on as a sub for John Robertson, who was later my assistant at various clubs in my career as a manager. I was 19 at the time and John was 18. Old Trafford was being rebuilt, but, even so, it was just incredible. I was playing against George Best, Bobby Charlton and Denis Law. Even though we lost, I thought – well, listen, I'm in business! I still wasn't anywhere near the sort of fitness that was expected. I was running before I could walk, really, but it was fantastic, because I was making a bit of a splash in the first few weeks without having had a pre-season like the other lads.

I think the excitement was carrying me through as much as anything else. Here I was, in England, for the first time living away from home. In those days the academy system was far less formal, but professional clubs had apprentices, which I sometimes felt was something I missed out on. It was a worry: at 19 I'd started playing relatively late, and there was a general feeling that if you hadn't made it by the age of 20, you probably never would.

These days you might feel like that by the age of 14. It would certainly be very unusual now for an undergraduate to be plucked out of university and start scoring goals in the Premier League. Football has changed a lot.

1

FITNESS

I have so many incredible memories as a player, winning the European Cup twice and captaining Northern Ireland at the World Cup. But one of the most memorable moments of my career is not so happy to look back on. It was in a game that took place at Meadow Lane on a bleak early February afternoon in 1985. That football ground had seen better days and better matches than that day. I was playing in midfield for Notts County, the oldest football league team in the world. Shrewsbury were proving tough nuts to crack, but outside of the stadium that day, nobody particularly cared. Just before half-time I stretched for a ball I could not possibly reach, making contact with an opposing player and falling in a heap. The pain was excruciating. I was carried off the pitch on an improvised stretcher; one of my teammates helping to carry it into the dressing room. The manager Richie Barker asked if I was fit to play in the second half, and the physiotherapist said, 'Absolutely not.' I tried to take the swelling down by getting into a cold bath. I did not know it at the time, but that was the end of my footballing career. I would not kick another ball in a competitive game. My career ended that afternoon. It had lasted 13-and-a-half years, from October 1971 when I signed with Nottingham Forest, to that day at Meadow Lane, less than 300 yards across the River Trent at Notts County.

That time really flew by. Did I really play against Bobby Charlton, Bobby Moore and Geoff Hurst, the heroes from 1966? Did I play, even fleetingly, with the mercurial George Best? What has happened to the game in those fast-flowing years, and what changes are still to come? Of all the many changes that happened in my half-century in football, one of the biggest shifts has been in the management of players' health: injuries, fitness and diet.

Injuries

Injuries are part of being a professional athlete. That has always been the case, and always will be. When I started out in the game in the early 1970s, most clubs would have a physiotherapist and that was about it. Brian Clough was my manager during the glorious spell at Nottingham Forest. For such an innovator, ironically he wasn't a big believer in the medical side of football, or at least that's how it seemed, because there was a period for a number of months when we didn't have a physiotherapist at all. Thankfully, common sense prevailed and success followed. Generally if you had a serious injury, you went to a doctor who was affiliated with the club, but he would not be full-time and would often be a GP. Scans would be very rare – perhaps you would have an X-ray for a very serious injury – but these days players get scans for even very minor injuries. The top clubs will have perhaps half a dozen physios at their disposal.

My greatest memory as a player was winning the European Cup in 1979 and 1980. For the second of those finals I played the whole 90 minutes as we beat Hamburg 1–0 in Madrid, with John Robertson scoring the only goal. The year before, though, when we had beaten Malmö 1–0 in Munich, with Trevor Francis scoring the winner, unfortunately I was injured. It was very frustrating because I had played the quarter-finals and semi-finals, including scoring in the away game at Grasshoppers Zurich in the quarter-final, but a couple of weeks later I'd developed a haematoma, an area of coagulated blood that gives you a dead leg, that got worse and worse. I couldn't bend my leg for 12 days. The injury came three weeks before the final and I had to seek medical attention outside of the club because things weren't improving. As I said, it was common in those days to just figure things out yourself. A former Forest player called Frank Wignall told me about a physiotherapist in Nottingham called Norman Collins, who was almost blind but a brilliant practitioner. There were only about ten days left to go before the European Cup final and I needed to do something. He said he could only see me at five o'clock in the morning because he was so busy. I accepted the times given to me, grateful that he would open his house so early and work so tirelessly for three hours at a time. Without his help I wouldn't have made the trip to Munich, let alone taken my place on the bench. And at least I was on the bench. I thought I had missed out on the opportunity of a lifetime through injury but, amazingly, a year later we won it again.

I was relatively lucky with injuries in my career until that fateful day at Meadow Lane. My injury was to a cruciate ligament, a career-threatening injury back in 1985. I should have gone to a surgeon quickly but didn't. These days players can have surgery on their cruciate ligament, and they can usually be playing again in under a year, but back then there was only one person in England doing that type of operation. It was a pretty common injury in American football but not so much in England. I injured myself in February, and in March the chairman of Notts County gave me away on a free transfer, which really shouldn't have happened. Between the club and the Professional Footballers' Association they should have been able to keep me on for at least another year to try to get back. I was trying to get fit earlier than I should have done and my knee kept giving way. I had no club to go to, but Howard Wilkinson, who was manager of Sheffield Wednesday at the time, invited me to their training ground. I would travel from Nottingham each day, and he would have a physio look after me. I did that for a couple of months but the knee simply couldn't hold. An operation was my only real chance but I had left it too late. Realising it was the end was a real low point because I was captain of Northern Ireland at the time, and the team went on to qualify for the World Cup again in 1986.

I would have been there with them had I got that operation more quickly.

That injury gave me long-term problems and has continued to bother me ever since. My knee is really troublesome these days and it all stems from that injury four decades ago. I could never play football again, let alone tennis or all sorts of other things I enjoyed doing. I like playing golf but can only get to about eight or nine holes before the pain becomes too much. It just flares up. It means I haven't kicked a ball properly since 1985. I sometimes joined in little games in training at Leicester with a big brace on, but not for long. I would play so badly because I would be running in a certain way all the time to protect the knee. I've lived with the pain for all these years, and tried to work around it, but it never really holds. I've even tried to play tennis with the brace on. One day I was playing after training at Leicester, with Steve Guppy, who was one of my players at Filbert Street. I was wearing my brace and tried to retrieve the ball but my knee buckled underneath me. I was lying in a heap but I tried to get the ball over the net, and did so, but then he won the point by just touching it over. I was lying on the floor and he was laughing. The last thing you want as a manager is to see a player laughing at you as you're lying on the ground!

If there's a consolation, though, it was that my injury happened when I was 32, not 22, so I got to have a great career. I was lucky. There were many brilliant careers cut short because of injuries that wouldn't be as bad nowadays, not least Brian Clough himself, who tore his cruciate ligaments in a game for Sunderland against Bury in 1962. He retired a couple of years later at the age of 29. Things have improved a lot. Medical treatment is much better now and clubs take more responsibility – a player wouldn't be left to make bad decisions like I did in putting off the surgery. I don't want anyone feeling sorry for me, though. I am far from the only former player to still be struggling with an injury, and, honestly, I look back and imagine that if you had told 19-year-old me at university in Belfast: 'By the end of your career you will be struggling to walk and be unable to do all the things you used to do, and your knee will be sore – but, by the way, you'll win the league and the European Cup,' I'd have bitten your hand off. If I ever feel pain in the night it certainly helps to think about that.

By the time I moved into management in the 1980s things were totally different when it came to injuries, especially in the later years. There were far more physiotherapists and club doctors who were always at the training ground, rather than people who occasionally dropped in among their other work. Even in the last decade or two things have changed a lot. When I was the manager of Aston Villa between 2006 and 2010 I think we had perhaps two physios and two masseurs. Nowadays there's practically a physio for every player at Premier League clubs, and so many masseurs too. Despite all that, players still go outside the club to get medical help. As I've said, when I was a player and had an injury I went outside to get some treatment, but if the club had found out about it they would have fined me, even though there wasn't always proper support inside the club. Nowadays, a player who's got the money will say, 'Listen, I know this doctor abroad and he's brilliant, and I'm going to go there.' But the team doctor might not agree with their diagnosis. All that has become an issue. I know this because it happened to me managing a team a few years ago. An injured player wanted to go abroad where he knew a doctor. I wanted to make sure the whole team knew he was paying for it himself. I was new at that point so I allowed it, but if I'd been there for a little while I probably wouldn't have done so. The player had ulterior motives for going out there. The injury was not that serious but he had downed tools and didn't want to play. Over the years, the attitude of the great players hasn't changed – they want to play, want to win, and are just as brilliant. But I do think the attitude of less great players has changed in that sense, and not for the better. Perhaps because the money is so good now. Even if you don't play or perform to the very best of your abilities, you can still get a very good wage. It is possible to have a bad attitude and still make a lot of money, but in the 1970s I don't think it was.

Another thing managers sometimes have to deal with when it comes to injuries is conflict between a manager and a physio. Managers generally want players back sooner, while physios want it to be later. As a manager it's always hard to judge whether concerns are genuine or whether physios are trying to protect themselves, because they are the ones who will get in trouble if a player comes back too soon and gets injured again, and they perhaps have less concern with results on the pitch than the manager. I honestly do not think I ever put a player on the pitch when both he and the physio said no, but if the player says he feels OK, and the physio says he could do with another week of rest, it becomes an issue, and it's hard to be sure of the right call. In the latter stages of my managerial career, players started to listen more to the physios and doctors who would be getting into their heads about injuries that maybe didn't really exist. The top players never want to miss a game. Even when they are injured they are saying to the physio, 'Tell them I'm OK. I want to play.' You have to overrule them sometimes, of course, but in later years I seemed to meet more players who didn't want to play, which was disappointing. And the matter isn't helped if the player has a huge entourage, because they have more people around them and as a result hear more conflicting views. Players are talking to physios about 'grade one', 'grade two' or 'grade three' injuries . . . but you can't always be that specific. It's an injury. You're going to be out for four weeks, if you're a good healer you might make it back more quickly.

That isn't to say that you shouldn't have all these resources if a club can afford them, but it can be excessive. I saw Brentford play Manchester United in the early 2020s and before kick-off I was watching the teams come out on to the pitch. Out came Manchester United's 11 players followed by a huge tracksuited brigade behind them, who took up two or three full rows in the dugout behind the manager. Some dugouts are expanding to make even more room. There is a wealth of staff behind teams now, and lots of these backroom staff end up in the dressing room. I wonder what they are all doing. They will each have their specialism and role but it seems like too many cooks to me.

Diet

For the modern day footballer who desires to make the big time, diet has become very important. Everyone is far more conscious of nutrition and sports science nowadays. When it comes to diet there have been improvements over time, from players eating steaks before a big game to the ultra-controlled world of player nutrition as it is now. Some of these developments have been good. This stuff does matter. But, again, I think it can all be a bit over the top.

When I was playing for Nottingham Forest under Brian Clough we would eat about three hours before kick-off, so a 3 p.m. game meant a midday meal. It was all seemingly less healthy back then. However, whatever was eaten back then did not prevent great players from performing at their best. Kenny Burns wasn't fussy about what he ate for pre-match nutrition but it didn't prevent him winning the Sports Writers' Player of the Year award in 1978 – the biggest sporting honour in the calendar year. The magnificent Brian Clough would very occasionally allow a beer or a glass of wine on the players' table before a match, possibly to relieve the tension the closer we got to winning a big trophy. I'm not sure any of the players participated in a tipple pre-match but the manager's psychology nevertheless prevailed.

I can honestly say there was never a drug mentioned in my time playing the game, but there was a lot of beer drinking, which there is a lot less of now. I would never drink beer after a match. My stomach couldn't take it. But lots of the lads would have a big session, especially if there was no midweek game. Players are now a lot more reserved in that sense. The games come so frequently at the top level that there isn't really time to go on a bender. Back then there was, or people thought there was. Would you believe it, there was even the odd player who smoked? John Robertson won two European Cups with me at Forest and was my assistant almost everywhere I went as a manager. He would always have a cigarette after playing a game. I think he started smoking just to help calm him down, and then it became habitual. John felt that the odd one wasn't going to do him any harm in the short term. The great Brazilian player Socrates smoked like a chimney, and that didn't stop him from being a great player, although he did die at 57.

Ironically some of the big drinkers were also brilliant players. Some had problems with alcohol, including Tony Adams, who played for Arsenal from 1983 to 2002. He was a brilliant player and could perform despite his problems, which was the amazing thing about him. Despite his constant battle with alcoholism, he became one of the greatest centre-backs England have ever produced. You don't hear of alcoholism in current players now. It would be extremely hard to perform at the top level with an alcohol problem. Still, there were a lot of games back then, and teams had smaller squads.

Although there was none of the sports science you get now, even back then players were always looking for the correct diet and wanted to eat things that would suit them. We gradually shifted from steaks to things like poached eggs, but it was far more up to us as individual players, the clubs were far less involved. I played lots of games having only eaten Corn Flakes before the match and ended up wondering why I had no energy with 15 minutes to go. That just wouldn't happen now – the player doesn't get a choice. Now, of course, I realise the importance of diet in maintaining fitness and prolonging a career. I wish I'd understood it better back then, but I suppose nobody really did. There was a lot of superstition too. Players might eat chicken once, and then if they played brilliantly in a game, they would think they should eat chicken again. I used to get cramp a lot, but then I started taking rehydration salts mixed with water. I found that helped me, but maybe it was all in my head. I used to be nervous before matches, so there were some things I couldn't eat. This still happens but now players have drinks and gels to get nutrients into them if they can't hold down proper food. When I was a player, we would never eat anything at half-time, just have a sugary drink. That wasn't some special isotonic drink, just regular orange squash.

By the time I was Ireland manager between 2013 and 2018, everything had changed. There was a whole routine of things given to players – gels, drinks, energy bars. Before the game, the table was full of stuff that the players could eat beforehand. I wish that had been available to me in my playing career. I think it does make a difference. There are nutritional reasons for it all, of course, but I think it is psychological as well. You feel like you're being looked after and that everything is being taken care of, and it's one less thing for the player to think about. If someone you trust says, 'This is proper food, this will sustain you, this will keep you going,' it might just give you a bit of a boost mentally as well as physically when your energy levels are dipping towards the end of a match.

Eating only Corn Flakes was one thing, but there were games I went into feeling nervous and didn't eat anything before a three o'clock kick-off. When I was a manager, if one of my players said he hadn't eaten anything, I would not be having that, but managers didn't get involved in nutrition and diet back then. There was more responsibility on players. Later in my career as a manager, when the players would be eating at a pre-match meeting, I'd be sitting down with them, eating at the same time, and you'd have staff taking care of all the nutritional aspects. The issue, of course, is that you can't completely monitor what footballers are eating when they're at home. There were always stories about Alex Ferguson employing private detectives to watch local restaurants. But ultimately you can't control everything the players do outside of work, and they've got to take some responsibility there.

Strength and Conditioning

I have to assume that the modern footballer is weighed regularly, as indeed was the case quite some years ago. Although the Monday morning 'curse of the weighing machine' as it was then known might degenerate into farce. A weekend's intake of food and drink, particularly if Saturday's result was excellent, might put the player over his allotted target weight and a fine might ensue. People looked for a friendly face within the medical staff to ignore the extra pounds that the weighing machine was making and not tell the absent coach when he came round to check later. Leniency at times was applied, particularly if the offending player had played brilliantly the previous Saturday afternoon.

It would be silly to deny that there have been huge physical improvements in players since my playing days, even if we all worked hard and put a lot of time and effort into getting fit. It's just a fact. In 1954, a couple of years after I was born, the first ever four-minute mile was run by Roger Bannister at the Oxford University running track. By the time I became a professional player in 1971, just a few people had run a four-minute mile. Now, more than 1,700 people have done it, and the world record is 3 minutes 43 seconds. It is obvious that athletes, including footballers, are more physically fit than in my day – there have been huge improvements in diet, training regimes and equipment. Players are fitter today because it is what is demanded of them, and they have the equipment, support and know-how to make them fitter. Does that mean they're better and more talented players, though? I think that's a debatable point. Those fortunate enough to see Law, Dent and Charlton might take another view.

Players do lots of gym work now. I was strong-legged but was never in the gym. I did plenty of fitness training and we did some 'spike work' too, on a Tuesday afternoon at Nottingham Forest, wearing running spikes and doing sprints. But this was nowhere near as popular as it would become later. Developments in fitness have enabled some modern players to have very long careers. Cristiano Ronaldo is a good example, playing at the top level in Europe well into his late-thirties, and scoring goals for Portugal after his fortieth birthday, while looking like a man in his twenties. But that is because of intense work, discipline and resources, all carried out in a way that just wasn't available to Bobby Charlton or Bobby Moore, who both retired from international football at the age of 32. If they'd had all the modern opportunities I'm sure that they would have gone on for longer. It is great that modern players can go on for so much longer. Life has changed and things have moved on. If I have a regret in the game, it's that I should have spent more time on the practice pitch. I should have spent time in the afternoons improving my left foot, my heading ability and my speed; I wish I'd done all that. I also wish I'd taken more rest. I was completely restless, all over the place all the time. I always felt my natural fitness would take care of itself, but it doesn't necessarily work like that.

Rest

Sleep is a big deal these days, in sports science and beyond. People talk about it far more, and understand how crucial a good night's sleep is to health and wellbeing, especially for top-level athletes. I've read that Erling Haaland wears special glasses in the evening to block out the light and tapes his mouth to promote nasal breathing. A little quaint, but given the number of goals he scores, it seems to work for him. Not everyone takes it that far but all players will be trying to get as much sleep as possible. People never thought about it too much when I was a player. Some people did recognise the importance of it, like Johnny Giles, the great Leeds United player, who apparently used to sleep in the afternoon straight after training. I was usually out and about with the lads in the afternoon, but sleep should have been more important to me. As a manager I was big on players staying in a hotel the night before games, even when we were playing at home. It gave them a better chance of sleeping well, particularly if they had young children in the house. When I was a player, though, money was tighter, and clubs only stayed in hotels for away games, and even then only if they were a long way away. For example, if Nottingham Forest had a game at Villa Park in Birmingham, which would take just over an hour now but be more like two hours back in the 1970s when there wasn't a proper motorway network linking the two cities, we wouldn't stay in a hotel overnight. We would leave the City Ground at 10.30 a.m. then stop off somewhere to have a pre-match meal. I would tell myself that on the coach I would catch up on some sleep, but it never seemed to happen. I always had far too much adrenaline running through me.

Sitting on a coach for hours on matchday can affect your performance, and sleeping badly does too. Mental health was never talked about at all in my day as a player, but I'm quite sure a number of players had serious problems. These days it is a subject that nobody is shying away from. I have had a bit of an education in it. A couple of players at clubs I managed explained things to me which I wasn't aware of. Beforehand, I held that limited view that because players are earning decent money they shouldn't have problems with their psychological health – but these players did. I learned quite a bit from just talking to them and listening to them as much as anything else. Nowadays mental health is much more openly talked about, which is a good thing.

Although players might be sleeping more, the top players in the modern game are not getting proper breaks between games and between seasons, which is becoming a serious issue. The club season feels longer and longer: for example, the Champions League adopting up to four extra games per team from the 2024–25 season onwards. Alongside that you have international breaks, and the summer World Cups and European Championships have expanded. Plus, pre-season tours keep getting longer and further away. Players are simply not getting to rest. Some only get about ten days off in the summer, which is just not enough after a long season, and they go into the new one still exhausted. The manager might decide they need a bit longer away from the pitch, but if you're a top player you're needed to win football matches, so it's hard for a manager to leave them out. This should be a decision made higher up and taken out of the hands of players and managers. Eventually, players are going to pick up more and more injuries because their muscles are so tired. Rodri is a classic example. He played a ridiculous number of games for Manchester City and Spain and then he got a terrible cruciate ligament injury. It's possible the injury could have happened without the overwork, but that can't have helped. It's happening more and more with the top players not getting any rest and becoming more and more prone to injuries. This may shorten the careers of some of these fantastic players who are playing a demanding number of games from a very young age. Take Neymar. He played very regularly from the age of 16 and eventually just kept getting injured and was past his best by his late twenties. English players like Bukayo Saka and Jude Bellingham have had such an intense workload from very early in their careers.

The addition of the Club World Cup to an already crowded calendar isn't helpful either. Players are playing far too many games these days, and this extra tournament will further increase players' workload and the demands on their fitness. People say players earn crazy amounts of money, which is true, but all the money in the world cannot heal tired muscles. Players are just not getting a rest. There are more international games too. I've seen it from both sides, as a club manager and an international manager. As a club manager you hate friendly international games. The Nations League has been an attempt to add a degree of competition and jeopardy to routine friendlies. It actually has some significance because it's how Georgia got through to Euro 2024 where they were the surprise package. As a club manager you would never want to stop players representing their country for meaningful matches, but other games you tend to dismiss as a waste of time. Yet as a manager of the national side, which I was, of course, with Ireland, you want your best players available because you've got a better chance of winning games. When you get the call from the club saying a player's not going to make it, that feels like a selfish act on behalf of the club.

I am not saying things were easy back in my day. For a start there were 22 teams in the top division, meaning four more games each season, before it was reduced to 20 in 1995, although there are still 24 teams in the three divisions below that. Back then there were some really intense periods, even more so than now at times. These days teams almost always have two clear days between games: if you play on a Thursday you won't play again until Sunday. But that is a relatively new thing – when I was playing, at the end of the season, if you were in the cups, things could get incredibly congested. In 1978–79 we were trying to win the league title for the second year in a row. We won the European Cup that season, of course, but came second in the league, eight points behind Liverpool. We only lost three games all season and Liverpool lost four, but we drew 18 out of 42 games, which killed us. In April we were putting a good run together and thought we might catch Liverpool. We beat Chelsea at home on a Saturday, then drew with Cologne in our massive European Cup semi-final in midweek, before we went third in the league after a 2–1 win against our big rivals Derby County on Saturday 14 April. You would see that sort of timetable nowadays. But after that things got crazy. We had so many games in a short space of time and simply couldn't keep up the pace. After the game on the Saturday, Leeds at home in the league was on Monday, then Manchester United on Wednesday. They were both top teams and we drew both, which ended our league chances. We were exhausted, more so than our opponents because of our European fixtures. In that sense the fixture congestion could be even worse than it is now.

The big difference between then and now, though, is that you would get a good amount of time off in the summer. There were international qualification matches in the summer sometimes, but in general we had a lot more time off and it did us good. These days teams have long pre-season tours, sometimes flying to Asia or North America. This is all quite new although we had one huge trip to North and South America after winning the European Cup, which I'll talk about in the next chapter. Brian Clough didn't join us on that trip. Clough was a believer in a relatively short pre-season. He always said, 'Football matches get you fit.' So we would maybe have one week of intense training, then a lot of friendly games before the season would start. I've been to other football clubs where the pre-season was longer and there were fewer games in the build-up to the new season, but you were doing intense physical work all the time. It was like that at Norwich and Manchester City. The training was very hard, including lots of running, which I never liked much. Back then there was a consensus that a long holiday would do you good and make you play better. Some of that has been lost now. We'd have pretty much four weeks off every summer, when you could go on a long holiday with your family and switch off a bit. Spain was the most common destination in those days, from the UK. I wouldn't do much exercise when I was there, you felt as if you were defeating the object of trying to get a break if you did.

In Scotland, where the winter is notably harsher than in England and games often get postponed, there has long been a debate about taking a winter break. Personally, I think it is a brilliant idea. Of the five years that I was there managing Celtic, we took a winter break in two of those years. We played matches until just after New Year, including the traditional games around Christmas, which the fans like. Then we had a three-week break. Psychologically, it was fantastic because when you started the season in summer, your mind was focusing not on the end of the season but on January and the upcoming break. Everyone would look forward to that, me as a manager and my players too. I don't think it's any coincidence that the year that we had a winter break we reached the UEFA Cup final. What I would normally do is give the lads a week off, which was particularly nice for the foreign players who might not have their immediate families in Glasgow so could go home and see their families and friends. After that we would all meet up in Florida for a week. Even though we knew we were coming back to a very chilly Scotland, it felt good. I really enjoyed those weeks in Florida: we would be training, the sun was shining, it was lovely to spend time with each other and it all felt a bit more relaxed. I'm absolutely convinced that the break did the lads good, both physically and mentally. I think there should be a proper winter break in England, but it feels like things are going in the other direction and the calendar is becoming more crowded than ever.

As the fixture calendar gets more and more packed, players also need to learn how to conserve energy within games, when to hold back and when to run as hard as they can. If you are pressing from an early stage, with your players running hard to try to get the ball back and close down, the opposition will know you can't sustain that for 90 minutes. It is just a physical impossibility. So, it's about knowing how and when to expend energy. You can conserve energy by holding off for a little while when the opposition have the ball, and also sometimes when you have possession. High-possession football has become very popular in recent years, and when it works well, the idea is that your passes, whether they're going forwards or backwards, should have a meaning and a purpose to them, which might be to give your forward players a break from pressing.

Looking back over how the world of fitness has changed since my time as a player, I have to say the changes have been mostly positive. It is easy to glamourise the past, but I wish I had known what I do now about the importance of nutrition and rest. My one big complaint about fitness in the modern game is the ridiculous fixture congestion, which only seems to be heading in one direction – and is having a negative impact on the sport because by the end of the season the best players are too exhausted to play to the best of their abilities, or are getting injured through overwork. For the most part, though, things are better now. It is fantastic that medical treatment has developed so much, even if I have my quibbles with all the fussing and extra staff. We now know all sorts of things that we didn't back then, although it's hard not to be a little nostalgic about the days of eating steak while winning the league.

2
GLOBALISATION

I only went on a plane once before I was 19 years old. I was doing A-level French and my brother was a teacher; he convinced me to go to Paris for a few days to help me prepare for the forthcoming examinations. I remember having a nightmare with my baggage while changing flights in London. When I finally got to France I got in a taxi and asked to visit an address my brother had given me, but the driver couldn't understand a word I was saying. I eventually met a bloke from Northampton who I spent the week with. I didn't learn a word of French. The next time I needed to fly was to cross the Irish Sea when I joined Nottingham Forest at the age of 19.

The world has got a lot smaller over the course of my lifetime. This is true of life in general and is especially true in football. International football predates me, of course. The first World Cup was in 1930 and the first European Cup in 1955–56. International fixtures were happening long before those two competitions, so players travelling abroad is nothing new, but there is far more of it now. Also, these days everyone who plays football in any country is far more influenced by what goes on elsewhere. This manifests itself in all sorts of ways – from the influx of foreign players into the Premier League to the ease of watching matches on TV around the world, meaning European clubs now have huge global followings. Opening up the English leagues to foreign influences and players has raised the level of the game. I have had opportunities to share a pitch and a dressing room with many incredible players from around the world. It makes the game more exciting for spectators and it raises the levels of domestic players too. But I've always thought it important that football retains the character of where it is played, be that in England, or in other countries too, rather than becoming a completely globalised game that feels the same everywhere. Overall, though, the internationalisation of football has been a positive development that has taught me all sorts of things, about football and the world in general.

Although most people didn't travel abroad much in the 1970s, as a footballer I was lucky in that I got to go to lots of cities, with Northern Ireland and Nottingham Forest. The experience of travelling overseas to play European games was hugely different to the way I would experience it later with Celtic and Aston Villa, and things have even changed in the years since then. The biggest difference is that in my playing days you would have far less knowledge of who you would be coming up against. Nowadays there are so many more games, and more on TV, that you will probably know lots about your opponents in advance. Access to data is at your fingertips today. If you don't catch a team on TV you can just get up videos and data on a computer in seconds. Another thing that made it feel remote back then was that when you played abroad there would be far fewer away fans than now, because travelling was so much harder and more expensive.

Adventures into the Unknown

Back then, winning the European Cup took just nine games: four two-legged knockout rounds followed by a final. This is far fewer games than now, especially since the expansion of the Champions League from the 2024–25 season. The team that wins plays 15 games, or 17 if they finish outside the top eight in the group stage so play an extra knockout round, and that's discounting any qualifying rounds which some teams play. This constant churn of fixtures does lessen the thrill of each game a bit. When I look back on my two European Cup-winning campaigns, all the trips abroad felt so momentous and exotic, and each time we were visiting somewhere that felt completely different, with a unique culture and style of football. It was a really singular opportunity to visit all sorts of places that otherwise I might never have seen, although I'm not sure that sightseeing was high on the agenda.

Each round was over two legs, one home and one away. Our first European game in the 1978–79 season was against Liverpool, not a long voyage by any stretch of the imagination, but a daunting task nevertheless because they were reigning

European Champions. However, by brilliant management, we defeated them. In the next round we went to Greece to play AEK Athens. As luck would have it, we had played a friendly at the same stadium a few months earlier, so that wasn't as daunting as it could have been, and we won again. In the quarter-final we played Grasshoppers Zurich in Switzerland. That was a massive game because having beaten Liverpool and then AEK Athens, both of whom we knew a bit about, this was a team about which we knew almost nothing. This wasn't some friendly, it was the quarter-final of the European Cup. I remember that trip to Switzerland as if it was yesterday. They had some really fine players. We had won 4–1 at the City Ground after scoring a couple of goals in the last few minutes, giving us some much needed breathing room, but the atmosphere there was really hostile considering there were only 18,000 fans or so. They scored a penalty after less than half an hour and for a brief period panic set in. A few minutes later, I remember assistant manager Peter Taylor shouting at me to get into the penalty box from the far side because John Robertson was making a break down the left-hand side, and I bundled the ball into the net to make it 1–1, and 5–2 to us on aggregate. It knocked the heart out of them and moments later we were in the semi-final.

These days there is a degree of standardisation in everything, so a UEFA game in some obscure corner of eastern Europe will to an extent look and feel similar to one played at Anfield or in the Bernabéu. I understand why – the TV product looks very professional wherever the game is played, and it is better for the spectator in many respects – although some of the charm is lost when everything feels so similar. The same is true at World Cups. When you look at old clips of tournaments it used to be instantly recognisable where the game was being played, with the balls, the adverts and the pitches giving a real sense of place, down to quirky details like the ticker tape that was everywhere in Argentina in 1978. But if you watch footage from any World Cup from the last 20 years or so, it all looks the same.

In that 1978–79 European Cup campaign, after Grasshoppers Zurich, we played Cologne at the City Ground. We knew they were a decent side. Peter Taylor had gone over to Germany to see them play beforehand and so we were aware that they had German internationals playing for them, and had received a few hints about their style of play, but essentially our knowledge of the team was pretty limited. Nowadays whoever your opposition may be, from the most obscure side you might play in an early European qualifying round to a pre-season friendly on the other side of the world, you can find out a lot. Even when someone went to watch a game, like Peter Taylor did before Cologne, we would have no idea if that game was representative, or affected by something like a last-minute tactical tweak, or an injury to a key player. This meant there were always surprises when we played foreign teams, no matter how much research we did. In the most atmospheric club game I think I have ever played, we were two goals down in the blink of an eye against Cologne. Only heart and resilience kept us in the tie, but fight back we did to actually get in front 3–2. A late Cologne equaliser was a major blow but not fatal. We just had to go to Germany and win the game. We managed to do it with a 1–0 victory in Cologne in what was another electric atmosphere. It was just an incredible experience: Nottingham Forest qualifying for the final of the European Cup. The record books show a 1–0 victory over Swedish club Malmö, with the East Midlands club pronounced the European Cup winners. That was maybe less of an adjustment than other games because both teams were playing on neutral turf, in Munich, so there wasn't the hostile atmosphere of an away game, but it was still way out of our comfort zone. What a feeling to lift the European Cup.

Cold War Football

In the 1979–80 season we were coming off the back of an incredible run of winning the First Division and European Cup in consecutive years, and I don't think anyone expected us to go and do it again. There were more culture shocks. The first team we beat was a Swedish side called Öster, then we took two trips behind the Iron Curtain to play Romanian side Argeş Piteşti and East German side Dynamo Berlin in the next rounds. This was during the Cold War between the USA and its allies including the UK, and the Soviet Union and its satellite states in eastern Europe – including Romania and East Germany. There were worries about nuclear weapons and espionage, and these places seemed remote and exotic. Few western Europeans travelled behind the Iron Curtain in those days, but, as footballers, we sort of stood outside of politics. The European Cup straddled the Iron Curtain and saw people from western Europe and eastern Europe interacting with each other in a way they didn't really anywhere else. Football can be funny like that. We certainly didn't realise it at the time but we got quite an insight into the world politics of that period. It didn't sink in until the end of my career how significant some of those experiences were. We won against Argeş Piteşti, who won the Romanian league three times in the 1970s but have fallen a long way since then. That was fairly comfortable, but the quarter-final game against Dynamo Berlin was a lot harder.

Of course back in those days Berlin, and Germany as a whole, was split into two halves, the East and the West. Dynamo played in the communist East and were essentially an East German army team. They were very good and beat us 1–0 at the City Ground, so things were stacked against us when we flew out there two weeks later. East Berlin was quite the experience. These days you can be confident of getting a good hotel wherever you go in Europe, even if you might have a bit of a drive on the day of the game. That wasn't true back then because there was very little tourism in East Berlin. Visiting East Germany from the UK or USA was heavily restricted, but football was one of the few things that spanned the Iron Curtain. The hotel we stayed in was absolutely terrible. There were all sorts of rumours about spies and the dressing rooms being bugged. It feels like something out of a film looking back on it all. We were completely unknown out there as well, which was a strange feeling at a time when we were major public figures in the UK, having recently won big trophies. I remember Brian Clough getting into a lift in the hotel with me and some other players. He was a celebrity in the UK by that point but the people in the lift had no idea who he was even though we had club tracksuits on. He remarked upon how amazing it was that people around the world live such different lives, and that outside our little bubble, people had other things to do rather than worrying about a football match the following day.

On the day of that game in East Berlin, it was mid-March but I remember it being absolutely freezing. It was about -7° and we had to walk about 300 yards from the dressing room to the pitch. There were soldiers all over the place; it was all a bit surreal. Back then East Germans were effectively kept in, with a wall in Berlin to stop people escaping to the west where there were better economic opportunities. Somehow, we won the match 3–1, which was an extraordinary achievement given that we had lost at home. Only a couple of teams had previously managed to come back from a home defeat to go through in the European Cup. That happens quite regularly now but winning away was more of an achievement then, because going away from home in Europe was so much more uncomfortable and more of a culture shock than it is now.

A quarter-final victory in East Berlin gave us renewed confidence going into the semi-final of the European Cup in April 1980, but we were fully aware that another home performance like the one we had just had against Dynamo Berlin would seriously damage our hopes of retaining that trophy we'd fought so hard to win the previous year.

Dutch champions Ajax, with Holland and Denmark international players in their squad, stood in the way of our progress to the Bernabéu Stadium in Madrid, where the final was taking place. Real Madrid were in the other semi-final against Hamburg of Germany and if they won they would play the final in front of their own fans. What an advantage that would be for them.

Our thoughts were light years away from Madrid, though. Ajax were a very good team indeed. In recent weeks Brian Clough had signed Stan Bowles, the wonderfully gifted footballer who'd been hero-worshipped at Queens Park Rangers. His talents were waning but Clough and Taylor believed that, even for a short while, he could give us that extra midfield creativity that might win us some big games, including the European Cup once more.

He started the first leg of the semi-final against Ajax at the City Ground at the expense of the vastly underrated Ian Bowyer, who could not only defend when necessary but could score goals as well, like in the previous year's semi-final in Cologne when we desperately needed one. Stan's ability on the ball could not be questioned, but he was never the best at winning possession, and found it hard when the Ajax team counter-attacked at the City Ground. In the circumstances he did well but the night belonged to Trevor Francis, back to his explosive best after a little lull in form by his high standards. He gave us a first-half lead, doubled in the second half with a goal neatly squeezed home by the imperious John Robertson. On the BBC highlights programme later that night, the commentator Barry Davies lamented that the City Ground, not for the first time on a European night, was not full to capacity. This was remarkable compared to recent years when, even when Forest were languishing in the Championship, the ground was practically full for every game.

The scoreline, 2–0, seemed a good one to take to Holland a fortnight later, but not one player thought it was over. Ajax had shown they would be formidable opponents at home. Within hours of the match ending we jetted off to the United Arab Emirates for nine days on a two-match tour, because our Saturday opponents Arsenal were playing an FA Cup semi-final. Brian Clough was a firm believer in a break in the sun, with relaxation the main thing on the agenda.

Back in Blighty we beat old rivals Derby County at the City Ground before heading to Amsterdam for the second leg of the European Cup semi-final. With the match less than 24 hours away, we were gathered in the foyer of our hotel, waiting for the manager, who had decided that we would stroll down the streets of the famous city, past the house where Anne Frank lived, and perhaps drop into a friendly pub if the players wished to do so.

We had walked less than 100 yards when three or four Dutch youths brandishing a small Union Jack flag confronted

Brian Clough, mouthing a few obscenities to boot. They then proceeded to set the flag on fire. Clough burst into action, whipped the burning flag from their grasp, threw it to the ground and stamped on it to extinguish the flames, at the same time defying the youths to step a little closer to him. They quickly turned on their heels and scampered away.

The manager was completely in his element and sarcastically thanked those closest to him for their 'assistance' in dealing with the situation. In truth, the incident was over within seconds but Clough's handling of the confrontation merely enhanced his reputation among the squad, if indeed it needed enhancing. We continued to walk down the streets, stumbling into Amsterdam's infamous Red Light District, wondering what the locals who may recognise this group of footballers might think of us.

What on earth was going on? Well, nothing, to be precise. We turned and headed back to the hotel in preparation for the following day's do-or-die encounter. Brian Clough had reinstated Ian Bowyer to our midfield in place of Stan Bowles and, boy, we needed him. His ability to tackle and win the ball shone through and, aided by some excellent defending, we reached half-time goalless with our two-goal advantage from the first leg still intact.

But the job was only half done. Ajax were far from out of the competition. The second half began with the Ajax supporters urging their team to break the deadlock. And they did, with over 25 minutes left to play. Ironically, just before they scored, Trevor Francis – of all people – missed a simple header to put the game beyond our opponents. But then, completely rejuvenated, they attacked incessantly, looking for that aggregate equalising goal. Those final 25 minutes lasted a lifetime. But the resilience, the willingness to help teammates, and the character of the team – ingredients inculcated over a number of incredibly successful seasons – won the day. When the final whistle blew we were in our second European Cup final. It was almost unbelievable for this provincial club.

If memory serves me correctly, relief at passing the Ajax test, more than unbridled joy, was the mood in the dressing room. Peter Taylor's pre-match comments that we would reach the final of the European Cup proved prophetic. But all that could wait. It was time to get our breath back and head back to Nottingham before travelling to Spain. Robin Hood would have been mightily proud of our achievement that evening.

The final was in Madrid. Our opponents were not the great club that called the Bernabéu their home but rather West German team Hamburg, who we beat 1–0 through a first-half John Robertson goal. After that we went out all night in the Spanish capital to celebrate. What a feeling that was. In four successive seasons we had won the Second Division, then the First Division, then the European Cup, not once but twice, making the memories of a lifetime in all sorts of places. I feel very lucky.

Around the World

I got to travel beyond Europe too. After we won the European Cup for the second time in 1980 we did a pre-season tour in some faraway places, as the club wanted to grow its reputation internationally. First we flew to Canada, where we played the Vancouver Whitecaps. This was billed as the European champions against the North American champions, but none of the Nottingham Forest team was particularly bothered after a long season which followed a relentless few years. It was all about making money for the club. We drew 1–1 in front of 28,000 Canadian fans and then played a game down in Florida against the Tampa Bay Rowdies which ended 0–0. We returned the favour by hosting them for a friendly at the City Ground in October, right in the thick of the Football League season. Can you imagine a manager agreeing to that now? We played Brighton away on the Saturday, hosted Tampa on the Monday, followed by West Brom on the Saturday. It was ridiculous squeezing in the Tampa fixture, but we won all three games!

After Tampa on that pre-season tour, we travelled on to Bogotá where we played the Colombian national side. The ground was thousands of feet above sea level, which none of us were accustomed to, and the Colombians were a lot more excited about the game than we were. There was a big crowd and a marching band – you can see footage on YouTube, although the camerawork is a bit dodgy. We were jetlagged, and exhausted on a deeper level after our back-to-back European wins, and lost the Colombia game badly. We were supposed to go to Quito in Ecuador the next day, but the game was called off very late. We were delighted because it was all too much travelling. In fact, we were annoyed with the whole thing, because there were no financial perks for the players, and Brian Clough wasn't even on the trip! Perhaps we wasted some of the opportunities that came our way, but it was just too long and too far and a case of bad timing. After the South American leg we still had to travel back to Canada for a game in Toronto. Alongside the game, our hotel organised a bus trip to Niagara Falls. We didn't particularly want to go but it was compulsory. We were playing cards in the back of the bus when it pulled up within half a mile of the Falls – you could hear the roar of the water, and look out the window of the coach and see this torrent coming down. The noise was phenomenal. It is a completely spectacular place but we didn't want to get off the bus because we were still playing cards. In the end I got off, but only briefly: I thought I was focusing on football in this period of my life and would go back to Niagara Falls another time. I didn't see rest and relaxation as important back then. Anyway, I've never been back to Niagara Falls. So even though I did a lot of travelling, I didn't always experience it to the full. At least I saw the falls briefly. I'm not sure some of my teammates did – I don't think Kenny Burns got off the bus!

After that we went back to Amsterdam where Ajax used to host a mini-tournament every year. I don't know why they invited us given we had only just beaten them in the semi-final of the European Cup! In the event, we didn't actually play Ajax. Our opponents were Bayern Munich and the Dutch side AZ Alkmaar. We lost both our games but I didn't care too much. We had done far too much travelling by that point. There were a couple of friendlies and we were exhausted before the next season began. It was a disappointing one given what we had just achieved – we came fifth in the league and didn't make it far in any of the cups.

I got to do lots of exciting travelling while playing with Northern Ireland too, most notably when captaining my country at the World Cup in Spain in 1982. We played two games in Zaragoza in the north-east of the country, drawing with Yugoslavia and Honduras, and then we stunned the hosts 1–0 in Valencia. That tournament had a second group stage and we drew with Austria in the Vicente Calderón stadium in Madrid, home of Atlético. We then lost 4–1 against France. It is hard not to wonder what might have been if my early goal hadn't been ruled out for offside. It was the end of the tournament for us, but we had made people proud back home.

Another trip that sticks in the mind was when I travelled to Australia with Northern Ireland. We went in June after the domestic season and played at the Sydney Cricket Ground. We also played in Melbourne and in Perth on the famous WACA cricket ground. We were there for about a fortnight, which ate into holiday time but it was worthwhile because I loved visiting those Australian cities – Sydney, Melbourne, Perth. Even though it was the middle of the winter I was walking down the street with just a light pullover. It was only a short trip and the quality of the Australian sides was low, but it really sticks in my mind because it was such a special opportunity to see somewhere so far away. I've never been back to Australia since. It's a cliché, but you really see the world playing football.

The most hostile place I played in was Turkey in 1983, towards the end of my international career. I was Northern Ireland captain at the time and the game was in Ankara in front of 35,000 passionate Turkish fans. The ground was full at least three hours before kick-off, which was very different to English football culture where fans generally like to arrive later and maybe have a drink and something to eat on the concourses, coming out into the stands at the last possible moment. British stadiums back then were awful compared to the facilities you see now (I'll talk about that more in chapter 8) but, even so, we were shocked by the 19 Mayis Stadium in Ankara. The toilet facilities were dire – just a hole in the ground. I'm not sure that would be allowed now. There were fences at the front of all the stands, and it felt like the fans were in cages being held back from us for our own safety. In England plenty of clubs would have made a lot of noise and you could have been a bit intimidated by it, but nothing came close to Turkey, where the fans were genuinely aggressive. The fences were ugly but you were grateful that they appeared to keep the fans away from the pitch. You expect to get abuse when you go abroad but those Turkish fans looked like they really wanted to do us harm. There have been big changes over the past few decades in that respect. There are still very hostile places to visit, for sure, and each country has its own footballing culture, but things are a bit more sanitised now. That's no bad thing – it wasn't good to have footballers and fans actively fearing they might get hurt when they went to a game.

Brits Abroad

As well as all the changes in teams playing each other overseas and what we might know about them before we got there, the increased movement of players across borders has been a massive change over the course of my career. There were few international transfers when I was starting out, and each league had a very domestic flavour. There was definitely a reluctance in my time among British players when it came to going abroad. It wasn't about money, because in those days there was as much money abroad as there was in England, even though English football is more lucrative now in general. It was more to do with the culture, and particularly language. There was a reluctance to learn foreign languages, and it would have been harder to get by without it than it might be now because English was less widely spoken abroad than it is today. Ian Rush, for example, struggled at Juventus, never really learning the language fluently. He later said the style of play didn't really suit him there.

Going abroad never appealed to me at the time, although, looking back, I'd like to have broadened my outlook. I was always inquisitive about other nations. I had A-level Latin, so learning Italian or Spanish would not have been a major difficulty. Perhaps it was some sort of inertia, because such a move just wasn't as common back then.

A few Brits went abroad to play and picked up new habits. Graeme Souness told me that he learned a lot from his time at Sampdoria in Italy. The team would do pre-season training in the mountains to improve their fitness. The players spent a lot more time away together too, which wasn't the done thing in England at the time. If an away game was on a Saturday they might be away from Wednesday or Thursday. Souness took a lot of this back to Liverpool when he became manager there, but the players couldn't get used to it. He attempted a lot of changes, but the players said, 'Graeme, when you were a player, you didn't do this.' And he admits himself now that it was too much too fast. Italian football was a very different culture, and Liverpool were doing well at the time. If you have a culture of having a few pints after matches, and you are the champions of Europe, why would you want to change things? Some things can be good for one team in one country but not easily translate to another – although, as I said, everything is more standardised now and the national differences are smaller. Liam Brady and Trevor Francis were other examples of British footballers making a success of things in Italy. Kevin Keegan was an international transfer that did work out: he did well at Hamburg, who we beat in the European Cup final in 1980, of course.

One international move I observed particularly closely: back in 1979 a shy, but self-confident young English footballer left British shores and signed for Cologne in Germany, then one of the biggest clubs in Europe. Tony Woodcock had experienced a whirlwind rise in English soccer. Within a few years of breaking into Nottingham Forest's first team he had won the prized First Division, the European Cup and was an established England striker at international level. Despite all this glory, he braved the elements and started a new life in that beautiful German city. His decision to do so was hastened by the fact that Brian Clough refused to give him the rise in wages that Tony was looking for in his contract. Cologne came calling and by the time Brian Clough relented and offered Tony the deal he was looking for, it was too late. Cologne, not Forest, became the beneficiary of Tony's brilliant talents.

Tony was very quiet as a young lad, but was starting to assert himself as a proper player when Cologne came in for him. He told me the biggest issue at the start was the language, but some of the players could speak English in the dressing room, which helped enormously. He went for German lessons pretty quickly and felt that was very important. Not all players do that. Gareth Bale got a lot of criticism from the Spanish press for never speaking the language in public despite being there a decade.

It is interesting now, many years later, to hear Tony look back fondly on his time in Germany, mastering the language which he felt was important for daily life there, and settling in with new teammates – players that he had actually played against in the European Cup semi-final the previous season. But equally as important were the coaches he worked with, the different styles of play adopted by them, their personalities and their motivational skills. Leaving such a genius in Brian Clough was probably a tough decision. What he learned from other brilliant minds was also educational.

Rinus Michels, then in charge at Cologne, was one such character. He is regarded as one of the greatest managers of all time. Named by FIFA in 1999 as the Coach of the Century, he is credited with the invention of the footballing style and tactics known as Total Football. Tony has never forgotten the coach's four bullet points. First, you had to be physically fit. Michels' constant running regimes were legendary. Second, you needed to understand how he wanted you to play, his tactics. Third, you had to get to grips quickly with your own game when playing. Fourth, always help your teammate. If you did all the above you would not drop below 80 per cent of your optimum game consistently, and you would win a lot of football matches if you stuck to those points. Michels once said to a brilliant German forward Klaus Allofs: 'I don't want 90 per cent from you one week and then three weeks of 60 per cent. That is no good to you, me or the team.'

The players did a lot of running in training, almost military-style. Because the German season had fewer games than the English league, there weren't many midweek games for them. Therefore Tuesday was the dreaded running day for the Cologne players: double running. So intense was the work that Tony recalled he had to go to bed between sessions to recover from the morning's workload.

Cologne had 16 international players on their books but none of them complained. I suppose they didn't dare say anything to Michels, although there were a few rumblings within the dressing room itself. When the German team had on the odd occasion two games in a week, they would call it an 'English week' because of all the games English teams used to play within days of each other.

And so, one of the greatest coaches in the game put extreme fitness at the top of his list of bullet points. I have heard on the grapevine that my one week of hard graft at Nottingham Forest pre-season training, during my time as manager, didn't go down too well with some of the nondescript players plying their trade in the Championship at that great football club. They told their agents, who told the chief executive, who listened to their complaints about distance running, or any running at all. I lost my job at the end of that week. Thankfully the club essentially saw through those players, and when Nottingham Forest clinched promotion to the Premier League some seasons later, those players had disappeared off the radar and hard work had been reintroduced. Thankfully his principles still live on.

Brits playing abroad still aren't all that common, although there has been a bit of an uptick in recent years. It has been interesting to see two of England's finest players – Harry Kane and Jude Bellingham – choose to go abroad, to Bayern Munich and Real Madrid respectively. Scott McTominay and Billy Gilmour, two

Scots, both played a big role in Napoli winning Serie A in the 2024–25 season. I watched quite a bit of Napoli that season and McTominay in particular was so impressive, getting up and down the pitch and scoring some hugely important goals. He won the league's player of the season, which is a remarkable achievement given few would have predicted that when he left Manchester United a year earlier. I am full of admiration for players who go abroad and make a success of it. I would say the Italian league has had quite a decline since its heyday in the 1980s and 1990s, when it was probably the biggest league in the world, but that isn't to take anything away from the achievement of McTominay and Gilmour.

Foreign Players in England

As someone from Northern Ireland I was quite unusual in the English league. Players from outside the UK and Ireland started to come to England during my final years at Forest. We signed a Swiss international player called Raimondo Ponte who had played well against us for Grasshoppers Zurich in the European Cup. That was often how you found out about foreign players back then, just like teams might sign a domestic player after encountering them in the cup. Ponte clearly impressed Brian Clough and Peter Taylor in that quarter-final, but the transfer didn't particularly work out. He was a talented footballer but maybe wasn't suited to the English league because he didn't stay very long. I think the pace of the game was too fast for him, which is a common issue for players coming to England from abroad. Lots manage to get to grips with it but I'm not sure he did. He was a lovely footballer, though. He left for France and then went back to Zurich.

Apart from that, Brian Clough and Peter Taylor never seemed particularly interested in signing foreign players. Taylor was in charge of scouting and he was the one that brought Peter Withe, Kenny Burns, Peter Shilton and Trevor Francis into the club. They were great players, all of them British. I think part of the reason for the lack of interest in foreign players was just the time involved. In those days you'd have to fly somewhere to scout a foreign player, and none of the stats and video footage were available, unlike now. Brian Clough and Peter Taylor also felt that British players were better at dealing with murky winters and bad pitches, and thought a foreign player might be a fine footballer overseas but wouldn't be able to hack it over here.

That stereotype was widely believed and there were almost no foreign players at all in England in my playing days, at the start at least. The Argentine pair who arrived at Tottenham after they won the 1978 World Cup – Ossie Ardiles and Ricky Villa – are remembered because the whole thing was so unusual. I remember playing against the duo on their debut at the City Ground; it was a great novelty back then playing against foreign players in England. Around the same time, Bobby Robson signed two Dutch players at Ipswich: Frans Thijssen and Arnold Mühren. Thijssen was a brilliant dribbler, an aspect of the game that really appealed to me as it was what I was trying to do. The ball never seemed to leave his feet, he could just weave past players and make things happen. He briefly ended up at Forest, although it was after my time. Mühren was a very different type of player, a brilliant passer of the ball, a little like David Beckham in the sense you always knew he would deliver in a great cross. The pair helped Robson's Ipswich win the UEFA Cup in 1981.

These four players helped change the stereotype that foreign players couldn't do well in England. I'm not sure Ricky Villa was a complete success but he scored a lovely goal in the FA Cup final, weaving in between lots of players, so I suppose it was all worth it for that alone. Ossie Ardiles, though, became a permanent fixture at Tottenham and became a bit of a cult figure, as did the two Dutch lads at Ipswich, contributing to the Tractor Boys' most successful period when they won a European trophy and almost won the league.

That was in the early 1980s, but the shift towards the situation we have now, where a typical Premier League line-up might have a minority of British players, is more recent than you might think. Amazingly, when the Premier League kicked off in 1992 there were only 13 players in the whole league from outside Britain and Ireland, and that was with 22 rather than 20 teams in the division. They included Eric Cantona at Leeds, as well as Peter Schmeichel and Andrei Kanchelskis at Manchester United. There has been a sea change in the decades since: most individual Premier League clubs today will have more foreign players in their squad than were in the entire league back then. Many of the early foreign players in England seemed to be Scandinavians, perhaps because of the stereotype that they were tough enough and could cope with the weather. Now players come from every corner of the globe.

In terms of foreign players coming to England, things really began to change in the mid-1990s. Dennis Bergkamp arrived at Arsenal in 1995 having had a tough time at Inter Milan, and became a brilliant, brilliant player. Bruce Rioch was the manager who signed him, but just a year later Arsène Wenger took over and stayed for 22 years. Wenger played a huge role in making English football more international with his knowledge of other countries, especially France. He brought all sorts of great players in. There was Thierry Henry of course, as well as Patrick Vieira and Robert Pires. Arsenal were the first to really build their team integrating foreign players. It worked. They had a brilliant side that won the double in the 1997–98 and 2001–02 seasons and won the league again after going unbeaten in 2003–04, which no team has managed since.

When great players come in and change the game and make it better, it makes English football more exciting and raises the levels across the board. The foreign influx has been good for the Premier League overall and is part of the reason why it is the best league in the world. One factor is imitation – if you are an English player and you watch someone like Thierry Henry come into the league with his blinding pace, you learn new things, and must raise your levels if you want to compete in the same league. You only have to ask Ian Wright to tell you how things improved at Arsenal once Bergkamp signed. It's not just raw ability, it's things like training methods too, and the way the foreign players live off the field. If you've got anything about you, and you see that example before you every single day in training, you'll want to try to improve. The level of the best English players has improved over the past 20 years as the best players in the world have started to play in the Premier League.

As a manager I had to adapt over time. I didn't have a single foreign player the whole time I was at Wycombe, but had lots at Leicester City, Celtic and Aston Villa. English football became more international very quickly throughout the 2000s and 2010s. The massive Sky TV deal in 1997 was a big driver because the revenue went up and the wages went up, so English clubs could sign the world's top players for the first time. There were some cultural differences with the overseas footballers but communication was never a big problem. The only players I've ever managed who I thought couldn't speak English were some of the English boys! Maybe it's different now, but I never had any need for translators in the dressing room, or anything like that. Players usually come in with basic English and they pick it up quickly when they're surrounded by it, especially at their young age. At Celtic I had Stiliyan Petrov, a Bulgarian, who didn't have a word of English at all when he arrived. But he tried his very best and after a year or so he was improving a lot. As long as you spoke slowly he'd be able to pick it up. He was a great lad, and now he does punditry on British TV, so that tells you all you need to know about his English.

Occasionally you'd think about languages a bit – like if you had a couple of French lads, they would naturally stick together, just like English lads would if they went abroad. That was OK to an extent, but you wouldn't want cliques to form. That's where I think the captain plays a role, not necessarily on matchdays but off the field. You want him to bring people together and make sure people are thinking about the team rather than just their little groups. Another big change that has happened is that there is now a lot more in place to help players settle in when they move to a new country. One of the things we had at Aston Villa, which I didn't have at Leicester in my early days, was a lady who would help new players settle in by showing them houses and helping with administrative things. She spoke French, which was helpful as that was the language many foreign arrivals were comfortable in, whether they were from France or a Francophone African country such as Senegal or Cameroon. Helping the player settle in is good, but you don't want the player to be totally and utterly dependent on club staff, phoning up at two o'clock in the morning saying they need something. It could be something really mundane like a player asking her to post a letter for him. That was not her job. They need to become responsible and self-sufficient over time, which is beneficial for them and for the team.

I had the privilege of managing lots of fantastic foreign players, from Henrik Larsson to John Carew, but I did always like the core of my team to be British and Irish, in the same way that if I was managing an Italian club I would want my core to be Italian. I liked having that domestic core at all my clubs – at Celtic too – because I felt if you're a manager and you're living and dying by weekly results, the chances of those players understanding how important it all is to the fans and the local community would be stronger than with the foreign lads coming in, who might take a little more time to absorb everything. That did not prevent me from signing foreign players, though, and I had some great ones, and lots of them were brilliantly passionate and well adapted to our football culture. It just sometimes helped to have British and Irish players around them. At Leicester I had my captain Steve Walsh, Robbie Savage, Steve Guppy whom I'd also managed at Wycombe, and Muzzy Izzet, who played internationally for Turkey but was originally from London. At Villa we had lots of great English players: Gabriel Agbonlahor was a local lad, then there was Ashley Young, Stewart Downing, Gareth Barry and James Milner. There was the core of an England national side there, but sadly we couldn't hang on to them all.

That was just my preference, but it isn't everyone's – lots of Premier League teams now barely have any British or Irish players at all. As far back as 1999, Chelsea were the first Premier League team to field a starting XI entirely made up of foreign players, only seven years after the league began with just a few foreign players in the whole league. Six years later Arsenal fielded an entire matchday squad consisting of players from overseas, including the five substitutes too. That was just a season after they went unbeaten, so it clearly worked for them. Both Chelsea and Arsenal had some fantastic English players in those periods, so perhaps those were quirky examples that came about because of injuries, but there have since been lots of cases of clubs fielding entirely foreign line-ups. The huge rise of international players is in many ways a positive thing, but the inevitable other side of the coin is the big fall in the proportion of English or British players making it to the top. Sometimes teams seem to have little connection with the place they represent. That doesn't mean all the players have to be local. The world has changed, and you have to move with that.

I talk about British and Irish players, but more often than not in the top division in England these days, that means English players. That has been a big shift: there are fewer players from Scotland, Wales, Northern Ireland and Ireland in the top English divisions now. In my playing days, every team in the First Division would have at least two or three Scots in the side, but that is not the case any more. In the 2024–25 Premier League season, if you look at the number of minutes played by each nationality, Scotland would rank 19th, behind Senegal and Norway. There were only a handful of Scots playing week in and week out in the league, including Andy Robertson at Liverpool, John McGinn at Aston Villa and Ryan Christie at Bournemouth. In my playing days you could have named dozens.

In February 2025, Liverpool drew 2–2 with Everton in the last Merseyside Derby at Goodison Park. It was the first time ever that Liverpool had fielded a side in the league without a single English player in the starting line-up. Many other clubs had done it before, but it was a first for Liverpool mainly because a couple of local lads, Trent Alexander-Arnold and Curtis Jones, were out injured. But football did not start in 1992, and it is an irritation to me when things are almost wiped from the history books because they occurred before the Premier League started. What is curious about that Liverpool fact is it was not actually the first time they fielded a starting line-up without a single English player. That happened in the 1986 FA Cup final when Liverpool beat Everton 3–1. They had Bruce Grobbelaar from Zimbabwe in goal, an Australian Craig Johnston, and Jan Mølby from Denmark. Of the other eight players there were four Scots – Kenny Dalglish, Alan Hansen, Steve Nicol and Kevin MacDonald – as well as three Irish in Ronnie Whelan, Jim Beglin and Mark Lawrenson, who grew up in England but played for Ireland because of family connections. The final non-Englishman was Ian Rush, a Welshman and Liverpool's record all-time goalscorer, who scored two against Everton that day. That game was an unusual one with eight players from the UK and Ireland but not England specifically, and it happened because of some injuries, but it does show you how well represented those other nationalities were back then. That culture of Scots and Irish doing well in the English leagues appears to be dying out, which is a shame. The simple reason is that there are far more overseas players because there is so much money in the Premier League, and that leaves less room for the Scots and Irish.

That was very much the culture at Nottingham Forest. I was a foreigner of sorts, being from Northern Ireland. For our first European Cup win in 1979 the starting line-up had eight Englishmen and three Scots. All 11 of Malmo's starting line-up were Swedish, and the whole bench too, although the manager was an Englishman, Bob Houghton. In the following year's final we had five Scots play – Kenny Burns, Frank Gray, John McGovern and John Robertson started, and John O'Hare came off the bench. There was me from Northern Ireland as well. We beat Hamburg from Germany, who had two foreigners – Ivan Buljan from Yugoslavia, as well as a more familiar face in Kevin Keegan, who had left Liverpool for Hamburg a couple of years earlier. He won the Ballon d'Or twice there, as well as winning the German title. He had won it with Liverpool a few years earlier, though.

More recently, when I think of foreign footballers that have come to England and really enhanced the league, there are so many names that come to mind. Of late, there's been Mohamed Salah and Erling Haaland, and before that Sergio Agüero, Thierry Henry and Eric Cantona. The best players in the world want to come to England now, and that is a good thing in many ways because it reflects the fact that the domestic game is of a very high quality. The same is true, maybe to a lesser extent, of Spain. I think one unfortunate consequence of all this though is the impact on other domestic leagues. In my European Cup runs with Forest we played teams like Grasshoppers Zurich, who had many of the best Swiss players, or Ajax who had lots of top players who represent the Netherlands. These days a lot of the best players from those countries play outside their domestic leagues, and those leagues have suffered as a result. It's all because of money. The best Yugoslav players I came up against in 1975 largely played in Yugoslavia, but that would not be the case now. The best players go to the best teams where they can earn the most. That isn't a criticism of those players, but it is a system which isn't necessarily benefiting football in the smaller countries where clubs can no longer compete with Europe's big boys.

I think diving has been imported from abroad. We always used to say that diving was something the Europeans did, but it is very widespread now, which can be pitiful to watch. That's not to say that only foreigners used to dive, but back in our day you had to have been nearly decapitated to get a penalty. Of course, there were exceptions. But diving was really frowned upon for the most part.

Foreign Managers

When it comes to management, there has been a huge shift in the number of British and Irish men in the dugout. There are far fewer English managers at the top level than in the recent past. Eddie Howe winning the League Cup with Newcastle was the first major trophy won by an English coach since Harry Redknapp at Portsmouth in 2008. There is a lot of scrutiny today, and coaches generally have to do well much lower down the pyramid to merit a go in the Premier League. The last English manager to win the top flight was Howard Wilkinson with Leeds in 1991–92, which was the last year of the old First Division. No English manager has ever won the Premier League, although most of the early ones were, of course, won by a Scot, Sir Alex Ferguson. There used to be far more Scottish managers – at one point in 2011, when I was managing Sunderland, seven out of 20 managers in the league (Ferguson, Alex McLeish, Paul Lambert, David Moyes, Kenny Dalglish, Steve Kean and Owen Coyle) were Scottish. Six years later there were none at all. David Moyes has managed West Ham and Everton in the time since, but it is a dramatic shift. Scots used to be dominant in English football, both on the pitch and in the dugout. My first three managers at Forest before Brian Clough were Scottish – Matt Gillies, Dave Mackay and Allan Brown. There was a huge tradition of Scots in management, and we have lost some of that.

That is not to say that there aren't huge positives about England's embrace of foreign managers. I was lucky to face off against some excellent ones like Arsène Wenger and José Mourinho, who both won the Premier League. Another hugely influential manager is, of course, Pep Guardiola, who arrived just after my time in the Premier League but has revolutionised the game tactically. Then there is Jürgen Klopp as well, who had some amazing battles with Guardiola.

These foreign managers have done a huge amount for British

football, and at times have taken things to a new tactical level that has really elevated the game. We don't have any modern homegrown equivalents of Ferguson, Klopp or Guardiola, or at least not yet. Some of the best English players in recent years, like Steven Gerrard and Wayne Rooney, have taken a lot of criticism in their managerial careers because they haven't got the results. But I do think there's sometimes a tendency to really criticise British managers, whereas there is sometimes more leniency towards those from abroad. A lot of foreign managers have stepped into jobs here that wouldn't have happened if the situation was reversed: an Englishman without many credentials going to work in Germany or Spain. Everybody around the world is attracted to the English game because of the money, and also because most people around Europe can speak a bit of English these days, whereas managing elsewhere in Europe might be harder for a lot of people as no language is spoken anywhere near as widely as English.

I feel as if the game in England has become a bit of a merry-go-round, with foreign managers coming in, and foreign agents controlling things, getting in the ear of the foreign owners who want to put their men in. Way back when Mourinho was doing brilliantly there were times when it felt that if you were Mourinho's taxi driver there'd be a decent chance that you would be put forward for a job as a football manager! You see these waves where people get jobs because they are connected to an elite manager. With Guardiola you have Mikel Arteta at Arsenal, who has done well, but some others haven't. It does feel like the pathway is drying up for British coaches, and I would like to see that change. For every Guardiola there are quite a number of failures. I do think there have been some downsides to how international things are now, and clubs have lost a bit of their local character.

When I look back on my time in football, one of the most dramatic changes has been how international the game has become, from when I started out from Northern Ireland as a foreigner in Nottingham, to now, when there might be ten or 15 different languages or nationalities in a dressing room. I have learned a lot from this shift, and not just about football, and sometimes without realising it at the time. For example, my debut for Northern Ireland in 1971 was against the Soviet Union, a country which no longer exists. Four years later I travelled with Northern Ireland to Belgrade where we played Yugoslavia, which also no longer exists. That Yugoslav side was fantastic. I think pound-for-pound they were probably as talented as any team in Europe at the time. What was interesting was that the game was played in Belgrade, where the local clubs had a fierce rivalry with Hajduk Split, and all the Hajduk players were getting booed by the fans. Fifteen years later, the Yugoslav wars broke out. Belgrade is the capital city of what is now Serbia, and Split is in Croatia, a completely different country. That is why those fans were booing their own players all those years ago, because for many Yugoslavs those ethnic differences were more pertinent than their Yugoslav identity, and the Serbs didn't see the Croatians as their compatriots. When I saw all that in the news, it was funny to look back on how a football match decades ago could tell me something interesting about the world we live in.

3

RULES

The footage of my second ever goal for Nottingham Forest is still available on YouTube. It was against Manchester United at Old Trafford in December 1971, the day of that terrible bombing in Belfast, shortly after my first goal against West Bromwich Albion. The video shows how football has changed in the intervening half century. In many ways it looks like a very different game to the one you see now. The pitch is far muddier and the billboards advertise long-forgotten local companies. The crowd is more tightly packed together because people are standing on terraces rather than sitting in seats. The kits look more basic with no sponsors, and are made of heavy cotton rather than high-tech materials. The broadcast quality is fuzzier and the camerawork jerkier.

On a fundamental level, though, things haven't changed that much. The pitch markings and the rules are pretty much the same. The competition is more or less identical to what we have now, even if the First Division has been rebranded the Premier League. While the mind naturally focuses on things that have changed, it is remarkable to observe how similar things have remained over such a long period of time. While we love arguing about the finer details of football, and can disagree passionately, the basics of it are almost unimprovable.

That being said, there have been changes to the rules since the start of my career. These include adjustments to the rules on the pitch – how the game is played and officiated – as well as the reformatting of leagues and competitions. Some changes have been unquestionably good. For example, if a football-loving child today was to go and watch a game from the 1980s, the biggest difference they would notice would be the absence of the back-pass rule. This came along in 1992 and completely changed how the game was played. The new rule banned the goalkeeper from using his hands if the ball was passed to him from one of his own players with their feet. (Heading it back to the keeper is still allowed, of course.) It was a necessary rule because back passes were making the game very dull to watch. The great Liverpool side that won so much in the 1970s and 1980s were masters of killing a game off by passing it back to the keeper. He would then hold on to it for a while before rolling it to another defender. If Liverpool were in front, and at Anfield they usually were, they could completely kill a game like that. It was very frustrating to play against. The rule change came in after the World Cup in Italy in 1990 where much of the football was very defensive and the back pass was used an awful lot. Banning it was a very good change that has made the game more interesting to play and watch. There have been other rule changes too, a lot of them for the better.

Refereeing

People do like to complain about how the game is less physical and more strictly policed than it was, but I'm unsure that's such a bad thing. Simply put, today's game is far less violent than it used to be. Some teams were so physical back in my day and did things that would earn you an instant red card now. In the early 1970s Leeds under Don Revie were the best team in the country, if not Europe, but had the nickname 'Dirty Leeds' for a reason. They could 'handle themselves'. Norman Hunter had a tough reputation – he didn't get the nickname 'Bites Yer Legs' for nothing. He could put the boot in. They were dirty but they were brilliant. I remember my first ever game for Nottingham Forest in October 1971 for the reserve side. I signed on the Wednesday and played on the Saturday against Leeds reserves. Terry Yorath, a tough-tackling Welsh midfielder, father of the presenter Gabby Logan, hit me right in the mouth and said, 'Welcome to the Football League', which was all part of the rough and tumble of the game back then. And it was just a reserve game! Of course, today with the video assistant referee (VAR), this would be spotted and the offender be issued a red card straight away. Back then, refereeing was far more lenient. Football was a much more physical game, particularly when teams came up against the most talented players. George

Best was getting kicked about every single week. We might remember a player like Lionel Messi very differently if he had been born a couple of decades earlier, because he would have been getting 'man-handled' with very little protection. Against some teams, you knew you would get a dig early on. There were still yellow and red cards but they were given out far less often. The best example to illustrate how football has changed in this light can be found by watching the 1974 Charity Shield, which saw Leeds, who Brian Clough managed for a short and disastrous spell, face off against Liverpool. The game was barely a football match, it was just boys throwing punches, mostly out of sight of the referee. Eventually Liverpool's Kevin Keegan and Leeds' Billy Bremner got sent off.

A big factor back then was the lack of cameras, which meant stuff could happen off the ball that the referee might genuinely have no idea about, let alone the fans following at home. Most games weren't on TV, but even in the ones that were, like that Charity Shield match, there were only a couple of cameras, unlike now when there are dozens covering every conceivable angle of the game. When I was playing for Nottingham Forest in 1977–78 we would have been on TV at most ten times that season, whereas now almost every game is televised, if not in the UK then elsewhere. If there are two lads having a fight you know it is being captured somewhere, maybe even by fans on their phones. These days you would just never get away with some of the stuff that went on in my time as a player. Even if the referee misses something, a player can always be disciplined afterwards. Back then, you might be on the other side of the pitch from where the action was and get an elbow to the face, and nobody would know about it. In some games there were battles going on everywhere. Ron Harris at Chelsea lived up to his nickname, 'Chopper'. It's easy to romanticise all of this and make it out to have been just a bit of fun, but I think the game is better now that it's less violent. There were some career-threatening tackles going on. It's no use saying sorry after you've broken someone's leg, or whatever the case may be. I think George Best would have scored 100 more goals if he had played a few decades later. He would skip past players, but often they would just take him out, or at least try to. A great example is a goal he scored in the League Cup against Chelsea in 1970, which you can watch online. It is 1–1, late in the game and the pitch is very heavy. Best gets played in and is bearing down on goal, and Ron 'Chopper' Harris tries to hack him down, but Best keeps his balance and slides the ball past the keeper.

There were far, far fewer yellow and red cards in general. I only got one red in my career, which came in a league match against Birmingham City in August 1980. Their left-back Mark Dennis was a really good player but also a tough one. In that game we were getting dug into each other, culminating in both of us getting sent off. Back then, red cards generally only came about when someone pretty much physically assaulted their opponent. There were far fewer second yellow cards too, and things like tactical fouls weren't nearly as harshly punished. That is why it was a big deal when Manchester United's Kevin Moran got a red card at Wembley in 1985, becoming the first person ever to get sent off in the FA Cup final, for a professional foul on Peter Reid of Everton. He took the player out when he was the last man, which is an automatic red if it's seen as a denial of a goalscoring opportunity. United still won, though, with a Norman Whiteside extra-time goal the decider.

To VAR or Not to VAR?

The biggest change in recent years has been video assistant refereeing, or VAR. I was finishing my managerial career just as it was coming in. It first appeared at the 2018 World Cup before filtering through to the Premier League and other competitions. I am frequently asked to talk about VAR debates in my life as a pundit, and I have mixed opinions on the whole thing. It has certainly changed how the game is played and officiated. It was obvious from the start that you would get far more penalties with VAR. People don't just suddenly stop holding on to players in the box because VAR is there. The difference is you can clearly see things now, whereas before when there was a scrum of players in the box it would be very hard to work out exactly who was pulling who. As a referee you're probably not going to be inclined to give a penalty unless it's really clear. Now with VAR, the referee can go to his monitor and watch it, and spot something that was not visible to the naked eye in real time. Often the footage is slowed down, and everything tends to look worse in slow motion.

It seems like VAR is here to stay despite the great many football fans who would like to get rid of it. The technology has been around for a few years now and there are still many frustrating aspects about it, but I think if it were to disappear you would get the same complaints going in the other direction. Unfortunate incidents would still happen because of human error and people would say, 'VAR could have changed that.' Imagine, after getting rid of VAR, a clearly offside goal deciding a cup final. That's why I don't think we will ever go back, even if it is flawed. It sometimes feels like referees are hiding behind it and no longer have the courage of their convictions. When they are asked to look at something again on the monitor they tend to overturn their original decision almost all of the time, when there have been a number of cases where they could easily have stood their ground and said, 'No.'

The offside rule has changed a fair bit over the years, and now with VAR there are some decisions that take a ridiculous amount of time to be reached. The big change was the shift from having three defenders between the player and the goal playing someone onside down to two, to encourage more attacking football. That happened in 1925, which is definitely before my time. But there have been smaller changes more recently which have mainly been good, I think. When I started playing, the offside rule took no notice of whether a player was 'interfering' with play. If a player was through on goal without stepping past the last defender, but one of his teammates was tying his shoelaces by the corner flag, that would have been given offside. That changed with new guidelines brought in in 2005 which said a player has to be 'interfering with play' to be considered offside. This can be a little confusing sometimes, because players can stand in an offside position right in front of the goalkeeper, and the officials have to determine if they're 'interfering' or not, which is a subjective call.

Overall, though, the change has been positive. There were a few occasions before that when a goal was ruled out because of a player who was nowhere near the action, and it felt really silly, although as the great Danny Blanchflower once said, 'If he's not interfering with play, what's he doing on the pitch?' The new rule is more ambiguous, though, and there are some marginal cases. There was an odd one involving Manchester United scoring against Manchester City in 2023, where Bruno Fernandes's goal was not ruled out even though it looked like Marcus Rashford was interfering with play, despite not touching the ball. You also get cases where two players go for a header, with one offside and not touching the ball, but causing a bit of mayhem for the defenders, and the officials have to make a decision. Before the rule change it was crystal clear, whereas now there is a lot more ambiguity.

There have been some big changes to the rules of the game since my time as a player, but perhaps not as big or as many as you might think. Football really is a simple game, which is the beauty of it. It is very easy for people to pick up the rules and start watching or playing. Not all sports are like that. I enjoy rugby union but the game is totally dependent on the whim of a referee. There are so many rules in that game, with many interpretations. Part of me thinks football is almost heading in that direction now, with referees being unable to referee because of all the other things going on. This started off with VAR and the possibility of it overruling him, but now he might feel that VAR is his friend and he can make a decision, and then somebody can fix it if he's messed up, which might make him less reliant on his own judgement over time.

As I noted, if VAR were not there, we might be in trouble: you do see the case for VAR when there is an injustice in a game where the technology is not used. In the FA Cup they haven't always used it in recent years, and in February 2025 Harry Maguire scored a late winner for Manchester United against Leicester City. He was a whole yard offside, which was immediately obvious from the replay. If you're used to watching the Premier League, at first you instinctively think VAR will overturn it but, of course, there was no VAR, and the goal stood. Maybe linesmen are so used to it that they are less inclined to stick their flags up because subconsciously they think they have the technology to fall back on, even when they don't. On the other hand, you get goals that are disallowed even when they look perfectly good on the replay, with the offside lines drawn, and whatever else. I think that if it's too tight to tell, you should go with the attacking side. It sometimes feels like the officials are looking for a reason to discount a goal that looked perfectly OK in real time. The counter-argument to that would be that even though a player is only half an inch offside, he's still offside. That is true, but when it's so tight, it can take a very long time to work it out, which kills the spontaneity of things. In the past a linesman would have to just make a call, and maybe sometimes that would be the wrong call, but in striving for perfection there is a lot you lose as well as gain. Celebrating a goal should be the most simple and joyous thing in the game, but some of that is being lost. This idea of celebrating once, then going back, then celebrating twice when the goal is actually confirmed – I don't like that. You often see a goal not being celebrated properly by players and fans because everyone is waiting for the signal from the referee.

Other Changes

One change that has come along in recent years might have altered the course of English football history had it been around earlier: goal-line technology. England winning the World Cup in 1966 had a big impact on the popularity of the game, not just in England but also in Northern Ireland where I grew up. It was a huge occasion and I remember it vividly; it certainly influenced my choice of career. On that day at Wembley, after 90 minutes the game was 2–2 so it went to extra-time. Ten minutes in, England striker Geoff Hurst controlled the ball in the penalty area and shot it against the crossbar. The ball bounced down . . . but did the whole of the ball cross the line? The referee thought so, or, more accurately, the 'Russian linesman', Tofiq Bahramov, who was actually from Azerbaijan. The goal was given and the rest is history – Hurst scored another in the dying seconds to make it 4–2 and England lifted their first and so far only World Cup. But did the ball cross the line? I'm not sure. Maybe it did. Maybe it didn't. You can watch the goal and decide for yourself.

Nowadays, of course, there would be no such uncertainty. Goal-line technology was approved in 2012 and was rolled out shortly afterwards, with little fuss compared to other changes we have seen. It was sadly too late for Frank Lampard. Against Germany in the 2010 World Cup his shot hit the crossbar and bounced a yard over the line but the goal wasn't given. There was also a shocker in the Premier League in January 2005 at Old Trafford. A long-range shot from Tottenham's Pedro Mendes was miles over the line before the ball was scooped out by United goalkeeper Roy Carroll, but the goal wasn't given there either. This would not happen now. One of the good things about goal-line decisions compared to other technology like VAR is the streamlined way the process works. If the whole of the ball crosses the line, the referee's watch vibrates. If it does not there is no vibration. This is good because it is fast, with no waiting around for minutes with no one on the pitch or in the stands knowing what is going on, which sometimes happens with VAR. A pet obsession of mine is corner kicks, which are supposed to be taken while some of the ball is inside the little arc in the corner of the pitch. I often note these days it is well outside the arc and players are sneaking an advantage. I would say the ball should be in the middle of the arc, not touching the sides, because that was what the line was brought in for way back.

Goal-line technology works, but it can't be used to fix everything else that annoys us about refereeing. It is so effective because goal-line decisions are completely black and white. The whole of the ball either crosses the line or it doesn't. Many aspects of football aren't like this. Was a tackle dangerous enough to merit a red card? Was a handball intentional? Was an offside player interfering in play? People can reasonably hold different opinions on these questions. We often demand the same kind of crystal clarity that goal-line technology can give in other situations, but this is never going to happen because so much of football is inherently subjective.

Although I've said I find the complexity of rugby union's rules frustrating, I do like the game, as well as American football and rugby league. I particularly enjoy rugby league because I think it puts football to shame in the sense that the lads get battered every single week, rather than going down and holding their faces when they're hit on the shoulder, as you often see footballers do. This play-acting is the major thing putting me off football at the moment. It's embarrassing. The same players who go down one week will be making a show of an opponent going down the next. It's worse than it's ever been. The referee is between a rock and a hard place. When somebody goes down and the referee waves play on, if the boy is down holding his face, the referee is almost duty-bound to stop the game because he will be in trouble if there is a genuine incident and the player cannot be treated quickly enough. Players abuse this, though. I really dislike all this diving and would advocate for the idea of some sort of retrospective punishment being introduced for when it is really clear that somebody is diving – cheating – and going against the spirit of the game.

One positive development is the increase in injury time we have seen recently. This all changed around the time of the 2022 Qatar World Cup. Before then, the referee would tend to just add on maybe two or three minutes at the end of a half, rarely longer than four, even if the ball had been out for long periods of time. Now they try to actually calculate how much time the ball has been out of play and add it on, even if it is ten minutes, which is a good thing if it reduces time wasting. I have long been of the opinion that the football authorities should take timekeeping out of the referee's hands completely, like they do in rugby where they stop the clock and start it again when the game restarts. This would mean totally removing the incentive for time wasting. I would be all for that. Teams are always wasting time, which to an extent is part of the game. I don't like it as a spectator or pundit but understand it from a manager's perspective. 'Game management' is what it's called; you would want your players to have an idea that if there are about five minutes left in the game, they should take time off the clock. If you're a goal up and a team is attacking you to try to get that equalising goal, you're going to want to take the ball into the corner, for example. A centre-forward might be wanting to get another goal to make it 2–0, but if the play breaks down, your opponents can break at you with your players out of position. It's better to just hang on to the ball and run down the clock. Similarly, you don't want your goalkeeper just booting it up-field when you've only got one player up, as then the ball is coming straight back to you. This is just common sense, really. Well-managed players will have an inbuilt time mechanism that means they're aware of all this. You don't want them doing it too early as, of course, you'd always like to get that second goal, then you can relax a lot more. It's also very important not to commit a foul. You know that the opposition players, the minute they're slightly touched, are going to go down, so you don't want to give them the opportunity to win a free-kick when time's running out. That is exactly what the opposition wants, and what you want when you are on the other side of the equation.

There have been a few changes to the game that haven't stuck around. An example is the golden goal, which was briefly brought in to attempt to make extra-time more exciting. Oliver Bierhoff scored the winner of the 1996 European Championship final for Germany against the Czech Republic. That was that, game over, no opportunity to equalise. The same happened in the same tournament four years later when David Trezeguet scored the winner for France against Italy. The golden goal rule didn't last long, though. It was meant to make things more exciting, but it was a bit of an anti-climax when extra-time ended after just a few minutes. Also it made teams ultra-defensive.

One other change that is maybe more positive is the increase in the number of substitutions permitted. Although players have far too many games now, at least they don't always play 90 minutes. During my playing career there was only one sub per team per game, which wasn't enough, but now it is five, which I am inclined to think is too many. Today it sometimes feels managers are making substitutions just for the sake of it – simply to avoid the common criticism that when a team loses a game it was because a manager didn't use their subs. But it doesn't feel right to me that you're potentially able to change half the outfield players. Generally speaking, you're putting people on to freshen things up, to hold on to a lead or come from behind, but it doesn't always work and can make the team weaker, because as a general rule you will have your best players on the pitch at the start. It is certainly more nuanced than a lot of pundits make out. A manager is made out to be a genius if a sub comes on and scores the winner, but that doesn't happen often.

Bad Decisions

Being on the receiving end of bad decisions is just part of football, and I have certainly benefited from some as well as lost out. But sometimes decisions really stick with you, particularly when it's not so much honest human error but the referee failing to follow the rule book. A poor decision I was on the receiving end of was in the 2010 League Cup final when my Aston Villa side played Manchester United. Nemanja Vidić pulled down Gabriel Agbonlahor in the box after just five minutes. He clearly should have been sent off because he was the last man. We still got the penalty and James Milner scored it, but Vidić stayed on the pitch. You often hear people say it's bad for spectators to have a red card so early on, especially in a cup final, but that's the rule and the referee did not apply it. We lost 2–1. Manchester United, with Sir Alex Ferguson in charge, could still have won a game with ten men, of course, but it would have been a lot harder for them. We had a lot of energy in our team with a lot of pace on the wings, and if we had been against ten men, Ferguson would have had to adjust, maybe taking a forward player off. But it stayed 11 versus 11, and Wayne Rooney came on as a substitute and scored the winner. I'm still annoyed about that decision after all these years. It was ludicrous. Winning that cup would have been a huge thing for us. My relationship with Villa owner Randy Lerner might have been reinvigorated and things might have panned out differently there. But, who knows? It's tempting to ruminate on the past but you can't change it.

I recall another big game when I was managing Celtic against Juventus in the Champions League in 2001, which was our very first time in the competition. It was at their place and the score was 2–2 going into the last minute. We were starting to think this was a fabulous result but then the referee gave a penalty to them for something that was clearly not a foul. They scored and we lost. I was banned from the dugout in the next European game against Porto because of my comments on the referee in that Juventus match. I was critical of the officials, and you always get into trouble for that. I had to manage the next game from the stand. That was the opening game of the Champions League group but it ended up being pivotal because we took nine points and didn't go through, which is unusual. If we had drawn that game we would have qualified. I did raise an eyebrow a few years later when Juventus were punished for some financial skulduggery and allegations of match-fixing. Obviously, there was no connection to our game, but given what had happened a few years earlier, it didn't sit well.

We beat Juventus 4–3 at Celtic Park in the last round of games that season, which was a very special night. Every time I speak to Chris Sutton he brings up that game because he scored a couple of goals that evening. That was a brilliant Juventus side as well, their goalscorers were Trezeguet and Alessandro Del Piero, and Pavel Nedvěd also started. Unfortunately, Porto won at Rosenborg so we finished third. The next year we got knocked out in the qualifying round by Basel of Switzerland before the group stages, which was hugely disappointing at the time, but we dropped into the UEFA Cup where we went on to reach the final. In 2003–04 we had a tricky group with Bayern Munich, Anderlecht and Lyon, who absolutely dominated French football at the time. We were brilliant at home, beating Lyon and Anderlecht and drawing 0–0 with Bayern, but we struggled away. We lost at Anderlecht and Munich so it all came down to the game in Lyon where we were big underdogs. We did really well, coming from behind twice to make it 2–2 with five minutes to go, which would have put us through on goal difference. But then our defender Bobo Baldé handled the ball in the area and they scored to make it 3–2 and put us out. It was really hard to take. We should have gone through the group stage on both those occasions, and if we'd got into the knockout stages we would have feared no one at home.

Another modern-day development is that these days, when you have a decision go against you, the coaching staff are all watching replays on screens seconds after it happens, so they can get a good idea if the decision was correct or not. In my time in management it wasn't like that. You would be far more in the dark, although you would often be in the ear of the fourth official. He can't do much about a decision that's just happened, but if you remind him often enough that the referee has dropped a few things, he might have a different opinion in the second half. Before they were wired up it was a bit futile, but now the fourth officials can speak to the referee during the game.

Competitions

As well as changes to rules and how the game is officiated, there have also been some big changes to the formats of competitions.

Perhaps the biggest change over the course of my career happened in 1981 with the introduction of three points for a league win, rather than the two points I had known for most of my playing career. It took until the mid-1990s for it to be rolled out in international tournaments. This change was a very good one. It encouraged attacking football because a win went from being twice as good as a draw to being three times as good, so there was more incentive to go for it, especially away from home where teams often set up in a very defensive way. The shift to three points also made it easier to catch up on your rivals if you started a season badly. You could close a six-point gap in two games rather than three. The season the change came in, I moved to Norwich City in the February, a few months after I had left Forest for a brief spell at Manchester City. Norwich were going for promotion to the First Division. We ended up coming third, a point ahead of Sheffield Wednesday in fourth, so we went up. We won 22 games and drew five, which gave us 71 points, but that would have been 49 under the old system. Wednesday won 20 games and drew ten, which was 70 points, but would have been 50 previously. So we got promoted, but wouldn't have done under the old rules, so I should be grateful for that! The change was also responsible for Blackburn Rovers winning the Premier League in 1994–95. If it had still been two points for a win, Manchester United would have pipped them on goal difference. Likewise, in 2021–22, when Manchester City beat Liverpool to the title by a point, Liverpool would have won under the old system.

There have also been some big changes in European competition. The European Cup was rebranded the Champions League in 1992. Before that the tournament was simply for all the teams in Europe that finished first in their league. Nottingham Forest qualified for the European Cup in 1978–79 because we won the English title the previous year. We won the European Cup, which automatically qualified us for the following year – the only spot reserved for a team who were not domestic champions. We then won the European Cup again, of course. These days there can be four or five teams from the same country in the Champions League, and it's possible for there to be even more – in the 2025–26 season there were six English teams because Tottenham Hotspur won the Europa League. Before 1992 there were also far fewer games in the European Cup, just four two-legged rounds then a final, and some obscure teams got to play big teams, like Progrès Niederkorn of Luxembourg who lost 12–0 on aggregate to Real Madrid in 1979. Teams like that would be in the Europa League or Europa Conference League now, if they qualified for Europe at all. The old system gave more glamorous games to clubs from smaller countries, meaning Irish and Northern Irish teams could play against the big boys as champions. For example, Linfield from Belfast reached the quarter-finals of the European Cup in 1966–67. For an English side, the European Cup was more difficult to get into than the modern Champions League, but possibly easier to win in the sense that there were only nine games. Also there was no seeding. This meant some of the big teams came up against each other early on, which doesn't happen so much now. You could play a minnow, or you could get Liverpool, like we did in the first round in 1978. They had qualified because they had just won the European Cup, while we had won the English title. Imagine that now: the two best teams in England playing in the first round of the Champions League over two legs in September, with one team getting knocked out after only playing a couple of games in the entire tournament. That was not very good for the money men – the main reason the format changed. People concluded football was leaving money on the table in the way it organised itself, and needed to professionalise, with the Champions League coming in the same year as the Premier League in England, in 1992. I do think the European Cup has lost something by no longer being just for champions. It feels strange that teams can win it after coming fifth domestically.

Another change is the away-goals rule, which was introduced in the mid-1960s in European competitions. The rule said that if a game was tied over two legs, away goals would count double. The idea was to encourage away sides to have a go and not just defend. They got rid of that in 2021. The argument was that home advantage lessened over time as pitches got better and travel got easier, and that the away goals rule encouraged home teams to play very defensively because they were so scared of conceding.

A new Champions League format was introduced in 2024. Again, the motive was more games on TV and thus more money, a big topic which we'll look at in detail in chapter 4. It also made it more likely for the big teams to play against each other in the group stages early on without necessarily knocking each other out. I don't mind the changes. The old format, barely changed since 1992, was getting tired. Under the new system, 24 teams go through to a knockout game, so if you're a club worth your salt you have a good chance of making it through after Christmastime. Lots of the games felt meaningless in the old Champions League system, but now there is more to latch on to, particularly for clubs like Celtic. In January 2025 I was a pundit at Villa Park watching two of my former clubs play each other for the first time ever. Villa won 4–2 but both went through to the knockouts. Villa hadn't played in the competition since 1983, the year after they won it. Celtic had been in the Champions League a lot but hadn't qualified for the knockouts for 11 years. Having 36 teams in the Champions League rather than 32, and 24 teams reaching the knockout stages rather than 16, offers big opportunities and exciting European nights for clubs who might otherwise not have them. In 2024–25 Celtic came 21st in the 36-team league, one place behind Juventus and one above Manchester City, which put them through, although they lost to Bayern Munich in the next round with a heartbreaking last-minute goal.

One thing that I think gets overlooked about the new Champions League system is that the lower seeds get a couple of easier games, which is beneficial. Under both systems there are four pots of seeds, ranked one to four, but in the old system if you were a pot-four team your six games would all be against teams in higher pots. But now there are two more games, and a pot-four team gets to play two games against pot-four teams as well as two against a team in each of the higher pots. Celtic were actually in pot three, so half of their games were against teams in the same or lower pots. They got a couple of easier opponents – Swiss team Young Boys and Slovan Bratislava from Slovakia – which they wouldn't have had under the old system. It's amazing to play the big teams, of course, but you also want some games you have a good chance of winning, and the new system gives you both. By the same token, the change does help the bigger clubs because they can have several slip-ups but still make it through. Back when it was a straight knockout you had to be on your mettle immediately, but that has changed completely. In 2024–25 Paris Saint-Germain only won one of their first five games, but went through to the knockouts where they were excellent, deservedly winning the tournament in style after thrashing Inter 5–0. Still, under the old system there were very few shocks, so the new system is an improvement overall.

UEFA introduced a new tier of competition, the Europa Conference League, in 2021. I'm not sure about it. European football always used to be something you were really striving for, but getting in the Conference League when you finish seventh? European football should be the pinnacle. If you're in it, you should absolutely go for it, like West Ham did when they won it in 2023, and Chelsea did two years later. Well done to them, but it can all feel a bit diluted. I suppose it's a bit like the new Champions League format where there's 36 teams and only 12 lose out, but for some reason I don't mind that as much – maybe that's my Celtic bias, because it suits them.

Although things in European competition have changed a fair bit, the changes are far less radical than the proposed European Super League, which would have seen six English clubs and ten others from around Europe peel off and form their own closed league. It was floated in 2021 but clubs backed down after a huge backlash. I was not in favour of that at all, and hope the conversation is settled, because it was really unpopular, seemingly with everyone. A proposal for a new competition which has ended up happening, though, is the expanded Club World Cup. It has existed for a long time but has been small and a bit of a sideshow, but FIFA massively expanded it in 2025.

Another way European football has changed is down to changing politics. As I touched on at the end of chapter 2, the geographical area once known as the Soviet Union now contains 15 different countries, including Russia, Ukraine and the Baltic states, each with its own league. The former Yugoslavia is now seven separate countries, including Slovenia, Serbia and most notably Croatia, who have really punched above their weight in football terms. All these new countries mean that the European Championships – the international tournament held every four years, rather than the club competition – has grown from four teams between

1960 and 1976, to eight in 1980, to 16 in 1996 and then 24 two decades later.

Play-offs

When it comes to domestic football and how it is organised, one big change has been the play-offs. My first full-time management job in 1990 was at Wycombe Wanderers in the Vauxhall Conference, now called the National League. In my first season we won the FA Trophy, and in my second we were runners-up in the league, which meant nothing back then because there were no play-offs. In my third season we came top and got promoted to the Football League for the first time, where the play-offs had been around for a while. In our first season we came fourth, which qualified us for the play-offs, a mini-tournament to decide one promotion space. We played Preston North End at Wembley. Their captain was David Moyes who would go on to manage Everton, Manchester United and West Ham. They also had Gareth Ainsworth, who would go on to manage Wycombe for more than a decade. We won the game 4–2, which was fantastic – reaching Division Two, now called League One, spelled amazing progress for Wycombe.

I have another very happy memory of the play-offs. After leaving Wycombe for Leicester (via Norwich) in 1995, I got my new club to the Division One play-offs in my first season, chasing the huge prize of taking Leicester to the Premier League.

We beat Stoke in the semi-finals, where Garry Parker scored the only goal over two legs. In the final at Wembley we beat Crystal Palace 2–1 after extra-time, with Steve Claridge getting the winner. I am a fan because it keeps your team going towards the end of the season. Before the play-offs just one or two teams went up in a league of 24, which could leave you with nothing to play for with a lot of games left to go.

Thinking back to my playing days and those weeks at the end of the season, one memory sticks out. Nottingham Forest were in the Second Division in the 1976–77 season and the top three went up – there were no play-offs. We started the season badly but then went on a good run towards the end of the season. On 7 May we beat Millwall 1–0 at the City Ground. It was our last game, but we had no idea if we were going up or not because there were plenty of games left for other teams to play. We all flew to Mallorca as there was nothing more we could do. Bolton were our rivals for that last promotion slot and still had three games to go when we finished, amazingly. The first they won against Cardiff, closing the gap to two points with two games to go at the time of two points for a win. We were very nervous. Thankfully, they lost the next game at Wolves, then drew to Bristol Rovers, so we finished a point above them. We got to celebrate promotion ten days after our season ended. Fixtures could be all over the place back then. Nowadays they are more evenly spaced out and the last fixture of the season is always played simultaneously.

That celebration in Mallorca was the beginning of a special

period – we went up to the First Division, won it, then won back-to-back European Cups. The calendar is a big problem now but it's easy to forget that, in some respects, it used to be even more crazy. The year we first won the European Cup in 1979 we played ten competitive games in April. Eight were in the league, of which we won four, and there were two European Cup semi-final games against Cologne. On top of all that we also had Lawrie McMenemy's testimonial against Southampton on 11 May. No manager would allow that now. The big difference, though, as I have noted, is that we had proper summer holidays.

When it comes to the domestic trophies, the FA Cup has lost some of its lustre, which is a shame because it was such a big thing when I was growing up. The FA Cup final was televised every year, and it was a big event, only rivalled by the European Cup if an English team had qualified for the final. I could reel off the FA Cup winners going all the way back to when I was a kid growing up in Northern Ireland. It sticks in my memory more than whoever won the league. Cup final day was the biggest day in the football calendar. It doesn't quite feel like that now, although it was very special to see Crystal Palace win it in 2025, their first ever major trophy. Part of the devaluing of cup competitions has come about because of the decline in replays – at the behest of managers of top clubs complaining about the fixture congestion, which is bad for smaller clubs because a replay can mean a massive payday and a moment in the spotlight. The replays did sometimes get excessive in my playing days, though. In the third round of the 1975 FA Cup – the round where top flight teams enter the competition – we were drawn against Tottenham Hotspur. We drew 1–1 at home then beat them 1–0 at their place in the replay. It was another trip to London in the next round as we were drawn against Fulham away. We drew 0–0. The replay at our place was 1–1 and nobody scored in extra-time so it went to another replay. In the third game it was 1–1 again, meaning another replay. Finally, at the City Ground, we lost the fourth game 2–1. You didn't mind playing all those games, though, because it was the FA Cup. Later, the rules were changed so there could only be one replay, which would be decided by a penalty shootout if needs be. From 2024 they ditched replays entirely from the fifth round onwards.

Women's Football

One of the more remarkable rule changes happened in the year I started my professional career – 1971. Unbelievably, women had been banned from playing on men's pitches for half a century until that point. The ban happened because women's football started booming during the First World War when the men went off to fight, and afterwards the men at the FA did not like it.

The ban was lifted in 1971 but even then the women's game felt quite marginal for many years, no thanks in part to that huge handicap it had faced. In the last ten years or so, though, things have really changed and you are now seeing some really big crowds, not just at the biggest tournaments but also at club games.

At the League Managers' Association Awards dinner in May 2025 I had the privilege of sharing a table with Jill Ellis, the chief football officer at FIFA who is enjoying her new role. In a previous life she was the incredibly successful coach of the USA women's soccer team from 2014 until 2019, winning two successive World Cups. It was, in fact, during the 2015 World Cup finals in Canada that I first took an interest in women's football.

Guided by Jill, the USA team looked an unstoppable force and indeed in the final they swamped an otherwise fine Japanese team with a four-goal blitz within the first 20 minutes, including a hat-trick from midfielder Carli Lloyd. Naturally the three-goal hero won the plaudits of the match but my attention was drawn to USA's centre-forward, Alex Morgan, who was just brilliant. Her ability to deal with the ball regardless of how it was played to her was utterly sublime.

At that time women's international competitions came round rather too infrequently and my interest, if truth be told, waned somewhat between World Cups. But, like many others, it was reawakened by the Lionesses' journey to glory in the European Championships in 2022 and then their splendid efforts in reaching the World Cup final a year later, only to lose to an extremely talented Spanish team.

But in July 2025 came sweet revenge. Under the leadership of Sarina Weigman, England's talented head coach, the tables were turned on the world champions. On a balmy summer evening in Basel, Switzerland, England retained the European Championship with a gritty, never-say-die, came-from-behind performance that unnerved Spain; eventually, winning the Lionesses' victory in a penalty shootout. Chloe Kelly, coming on before half-time for the injured Lauren James, changed the course of the final with her positive darting runs. In the shootout itself, a heroine emerged. Hannah Hampton, England's new goalkeeper, made crucial saves to win the day. Following the escapades of the previous few years, the Lionesses have taken their place in football's history books.

Players like Mary Earps, Lucy Bronze, Leah Williamson, Keira Walsh and Beth Mead have become household names in the last few years, and with major strides having been taken in the last decade there is universal excitement for upcoming major tournaments. At club level, I watch a fair bit of the Women's Super League, and Arsenal's exploits in the 2024–25 Champions League were extraordinary to follow. Their magnificent display in Lyon in the semi-final, overcoming a first-leg deficit, paved the way for a steely performance in the final to beat the strongly fancied Barcelona team. The women's domestic league seems to get stronger with each passing season, and interest in women's football keeps growing.

To conclude, the rules of football have changed a fair bit since the start of my playing days, and not just because women as well as men are now playing the game professionally to a very high standard. I'm sure Brian Clough and Bill Shankly would be baffled by VAR and the strict officiating that goes on now, but the reduction in dangerous tackles is a good thing. Football was aggressive and physical in my day, now it is more about skill, and that is all positive. It can sometimes feel like the game now is over-refereed, though. I like to see the game flow, not have long pauses for VAR. As I've said already, perhaps the most remarkable thing is not how much football has changed, but how little. Although there would be much to surprise a visitor from the 1970s or earlier, they would instantly grasp what is going on.

4

MONEY

One weekday night way up in Yorkshire somewhere, on a long drive home in 1989, I realised my time as a part-time manager with a career outside of football simply could not continue. I had left my playing career behind and was at lowly Shepshed Charterhouse, a Leicestershire club many divisions below the football league, while also working full-time as a pensions manager. I was still living in Nottingham, and on that 50- or 60-mile drive home from that away game in Yorkshire I realised I just couldn't do both things, even though my options were limited. Financially, even as someone who had won a couple of European Cups and captained my country, I had needed to get a job after my playing career ended. I had a family to support, including my two young daughters. When that cruciate ligament injury at Notts County in my early thirties ended my playing days, I had needed to find a new way to earn a living, and one of my former Northern Ireland teammates, Sammy Nelson, had moved into pensions. The group he was working with had a Nottingham branch, and he helped me find a job. I stayed there for a little while, and when the main boss left they put me in charge. I was grateful for the job and did my best. Essentially, it involved man-management and it taught me some useful skills I would later use in football. It was the only time I have worked outside football in my life. I hadn't yet thought too deeply about moving into football management, but I ended up doing so part-time, first at Grantham Town and then Shepshed Charterhouse. Football was my passion and had been my life up to that point in the eighties, and I just couldn't imagine spending the coming decades outside of that world.

A huge financial shift has taken place in football in the decades since I retired as a player. What I earned back then was a fraction of what players earn now – not just the ones who win European Cups but also players who are on the fringes of Premier League squads. I am certainly not complaining. I earned decent money, making memories for a lifetime. But it is a simple fact that there has been a sea change in the role money has played in football. Put simply there is just far more of it around. Some of that is positive, because players deserve to get more of the pie than they were getting in my playing days, but it can feel excessive, especially at a time when ordinary fans are being priced out of the game. If I had started my career a few decades later I never would have had to take that job in pensions, at least if I had been sensible with my money.

My first football job was in radio, working as a commentator and a pundit for the BBC and other broadcasters. That didn't involve the prestigious top-flight and European games I would cover later in my broadcasting career, rather, it required a lot of travelling to unglamorous games around the country and sitting on cold gantries. But I loved it. I enjoyed being back in the world of football after a few years out, but I wanted to move towards management. I achieved this in 1990, securing my first job at Wycombe Wanderers, which meant moving my wife and our two young daughters down from Nottingham, the city that had been my home for 19 years, to Buckinghamshire, just outside London. English football has traditionally been professional in the top four divisions of the football league, but semi-professional in the fifth-tier Conference, now the National League, where Wycombe were at the time. Part of my job was also to coach schools after classes finished, but I never really took to it. The chairman, Ivor Beeks, was very good to me and, after a while, he told me not to worry about that, and said we should put all our energy into trying to get promoted into the Football League, which would mean turning professional and a huge shift in the stature of the club. He asked me to go full-time even though the players were only in two nights a week for training and the match on a Saturday. It increased the pressure a little. The sooner we could get the team into the Football League the better, so I poured everything into it. It was the beginning of the best part of three decades as a full-time professional football manager.

I had a great time at Wycombe, although I discovered reaching the Football League wasn't easy. Only one team got promoted from the Conference in those days. As I mentioned earlier, in my first season we won the FA Trophy, a tournament for non-league clubs, and it meant lifting the cup at Wembley which was a very special moment for our supporters. Around 25,000 Wycombe fans had made the trip to Wembley, with over 30,000 total at the game. The next year in the league we got close to promotion, finishing on 94 points, the same as Colchester, who unlike us were a full-time team. Unfortunately, they had the better goal difference. The third year we won the league and finally got promoted. It was an incredible feeling, and a massive moment for the town and community as well as the club. The good times kept rolling: we were promoted again the following season to Division Two, the third tier of English football. It had been an amazing journey, but I couldn't say no when Norwich City offered me a job, though I only stayed there for six months. I didn't get on well with the chairman, and when Leicester came the choice was obvious, and I stayed there for five years.

In my time at Wycombe I learned things about management which I also applied to higher levels of the game. One thing I learned is that you might think at first that you should treat everyone the same, but that isn't always possible. The money players earn can be a big part of that.

The Flood of Cash

Salaries in football went up hugely during my time in management. The big shift was the boom in TV revenues that began in the 1990s. Chief executive Richard Scudamore did well negotiating for the Premier League with Sky TV, and the numbers kept going up and up as the game grew in popularity domestically, with football shedding the grubby, even violent reputation it had picked up in the 1980s. England reaching the semi-final of Italia '90, and the same stage at Euro '96, played a role in making it mainstream again. Later on there was more and more interest internationally as well, which meant more people wanted to watch football on TV and so the money got bigger and bigger, and pretty much all of this went to players, which strengthened their power. That was not a bad thing in principle. When I started in the game, the players had no say whatsoever. A player could walk in on a Monday morning and then a manager call him in and tell him he was leaving. Peter Withe was a brilliant centre-forward for us at Nottingham Forest and was looking for a small raise which he richly deserved. He had been asking for a raise all summer but Brian Clough decided against that, for his own reasons. Withe walked in one Monday thinking he was going to get a new contract, then Clough told him that Newcastle manager Bill McGarry was waiting to sign him. Withe said he didn't want to leave, but he had little say in the matter. Ironically, after Newcastle he went to Aston Villa, where he scored the winning goal in the 1982 European Cup final, so it worked out OK for him in the end.

A couple of years ago I was speaking to Nigel Clough, the son of Brian, who has had a successful career in management too. He said the one thing his father regretted was not financially looking after the players who had done well for him. He was always trying to be frugal with his existing players, yet could financially reward a new player who had never kicked a ball for the team. Today the player and the agent have more power when it comes to financial negotiations, whereas in those days it was the club who held the upper hand.

When the Premier League kicked off in 1992 I don't think we all realised what a big deal it would become, it just seemed like an administrative thing – although it was a big deal that fans had to pay to watch football on TV for the first time. The game itself didn't really change at first – it was the same teams and players – but it opened the floodgates to far more money coming in. I thought it was a good thing in general because the players certainly deserved more money. The 1966 World Cup win had had a big impact on attendances in England but not much of that cash flowed to the players, and a lot of those heroes of 1966 died without ever making that much money. Football went through a bit of a rut financially in the 1970s and 1980s when there was a dip in crowds, in part due to shoddy stadiums and hooliganism. Then along came the money, not just from TV, but also from other sources like commercial sponsorship, which ballooned around the same time.

Revenues kept rising and rising. In the 2023–24 season, Sheffield United, who came bottom of the Premier League, received £109.7 million from TV revenue. Manchester City earned the most with £175.9 million. The biggest clubs earn lots more money from other sources too: European TV money, big commercial deals, hospitality in stadiums. This has been an extremely dramatic change, and not just for the biggest clubs. Those TV deals changed everything. A lot of that is due to the huge international growth of the Premier League. It was very much a domestic league back in my day. Although there is more money coming into the game now, there is more going out too, mostly in wages, so the stakes are so much higher if things go wrong, and clubs can find themselves in a lot of trouble very quickly.

As well as the surge in TV money that began in the 1990s, some big club takeovers in the 2000s resulted in a huge influx of money into the Premier League, which in turn had a big impact on other clubs too. Manchester City were bought by the Abu Dhabi United Group in 2008. That was not good for Aston Villa, who I was managing at the time. We lost Gareth Barry to City and then James Milner a year later. With Manchester City's 'new' money, both players could earn more and felt that it put City in a stronger position to win big trophies. They were proved to be right. You try to reassure yourself by saying, 'Well, if Aston Villa succumb to Manchester City, it might mean that Blackburn Rovers have to succumb to Aston Villa, or something.' It's like a food chain, and you'd always rather be higher up. The money became huge around that time. Before Manchester City, of course, you had Russian oligarch Roman Abramovich buying Chelsea in 2003, spending crazy money and winning the league several times, which Chelsea had only done once in their history before he came along. (Abramovich was forced to sell the club in 2022 when he was sanctioned as part of the UK Government's response to the Russian invasion of Ukraine because of his alleged ties to Putin.) Then, even more recently, in 2021, Saudi Arabia's Public Investment Fund bought Newcastle United.

Nation states getting involved in football clubs is a game-changer, because they have virtually bottomless pockets, so it is nearly impossible to compete with them if you are trying to run a relatively sustainable business. There are now financial rules in place to level the playing field a bit – so the likes of Newcastle can't just spend billions straight away – but, over time, money talks, and the richer clubs generally win more games and more trophies. It's hard to imagine now what we achieved with Nottingham Forest all those years ago, getting promoted and immediately winning the league, then the European Cup twice. Of course, Leicester City won the Premier League in 2015–16, which was perhaps the biggest shock in modern football history, but it is very hard to envisage something similar happening again as the financial gulf between the haves and have-nots has got significantly wider in the years since.

It's hard to escape politics in football these days. Some of the owners I worked for were interesting characters, but now things are totally different and football clubs play a role in politics that goes far beyond the game. As well as Abu Dhabi and Manchester City we've had Qatar hosting the 2022 World Cup and Qatar Sports Investment owning Paris Saint-Germain. Saudi Arabia Public Investment Fund bought Newcastle, and the country also won the right to host the 2034 World Cup, bringing up all sorts of questions about human rights and sportswashing. You can't get away from this sort of thing now. Saudi Arabia's move into football has been significant, involving the signing of big-name players for their domestic league. I am in favour of investment in football in general. The tone of some of the conversations frustrates me, though. I don't have too much of a problem with players going to play in Saudi Arabia, if that's what's best for their careers. But there is far too much haziness about the rules, with clubs still having to defend themselves years after alleged offences, and teams like Forest and Everton getting points deductions in 2024. It is all getting very messy.

Agents

Agents are a huge driver of the constant upward spiral of money in the game. Two of the most influential men in football in recent years were international super-agents: Jorge Mendes from Portugal and the Italian Mino Raiola, who died in 2022. These are men who, at the peak of their careers, few of even the most ardent football fans could have picked out of a line-up, but they have had a huge impact on the game. They saw an opportunity and a niche at a time the TV money was going through the roof, and got hold of some players who did well and, the next thing you knew, they had lots of them on their books. As an agent these days, if you've got just one or two good players you can earn an extraordinary living from football, which wasn't the case not so long ago, when agents were far more peripheral figures. Ultimately there is more money in the game, and more is being asked of fans in terms of TV subscriptions and ticket prices, which keep going up and up. Most of that cash goes straight out the other side on players' wages and agents' fees.

There weren't that many agents in the game at all when I was playing. Peter Shilton was among the few players who had one but, in general, even in a European Cup-winning team like Forest, it was rare to have an agent, which meant clubs could treat players pretty much however they wanted. This had its downsides, because we probably deserved more money than we were getting, and we were the people ultimately winning the European Cups.

I found as a manager, and I still think that good players are never that difficult to handle. Their attitude is good, they want to play, and they are generally happy. They might have wanted more money, and the agent would come in and say so. And sometimes you didn't mind paying more to the boys who performed well. But I did get irritated by agents coming in and saying a player who hasn't been in the side deserves to be bettter paid. Whatever happened to the phrase 'chose the right time to ask for more'?

You also have to deal with agents getting in players' ears, as well as other clubs talking to your players under your nose. People used to talk a lot about 'tapping up' – when a club goes over another's head to approach a player. Chelsea got into a lot of trouble over it when they signed Ashley Cole from

Arsenal. Nowadays it is very common though for a club to 'agree personal terms' with a player before any transfer bid has been accepted, and in lots of cases the player never actually completes the move. It is supposed to be illegal, but it happens all the time. As long as it's all kept confidential the deal can be fairly smooth, but if it spills out into the media, you might have an issue.

Gareth Barry's transfer is an example here. He was my captain at Aston Villa, he had been at the club for a decade and was hugely popular with the fans. Liverpool wanted to buy him and Barry then did an interview where he made it clear he wanted to go to Anfield. But Liverpool didn't want to pay any more than £8 million, and we wanted £10 million, so it didn't happen. Gareth became frustrated because Liverpool wouldn't go the extra two million for him, so the deal fell through. A week later Liverpool paid £20 million for Robbie Keane. The story didn't find favour with the Villa fans, but Gareth put the disappointment aside and had a brilliant season for Villa. He ended up going to Man City the following year for £12 million, so Villa did all right out of it, and so did he – he got a Premier League and FA Cup winner's medal. I was unhappy because I felt we had a decent enough relationship and he was the captain of the side at the time. I think he regretted it at the end because not only did he sour his relationship, at least for a short while, with the fans of a club he had been at for so long, it all probably wasn't necessary too, if he wanted a move. He should have come to me before doing an interview with a journalist and explained he wanted to go to Liverpool. We'd have said, 'We'd rather you didn't, but OK, if they pay a certain price.' Randy Lerner would set that price, in conversation with his senior staff.

You are always part of a food chain at any club, with the exception of the handful of very biggest clubs in the world. Just as you might be looking over your shoulder at clubs with a bigger name or more money wanting one of your players, you would be looking at smaller clubs with less money and be thinking about which one of theirs you might be able to attract. In Scotland, Celtic and Rangers continue to be the dominant forces, but you must respect the other clubs that have less resources at their disposal.

Wages

I can't complain about what I earned in my career, but it was far, far less than what players earn now, even when you account for inflation and the changing cost of living. I had a house in a nice area of Nottingham that I put a lot of money into, and I often wondered at the time whether I could really afford it or not. No Premier League player would be wondering that now. Many have huge houses and plenty of other material possessions, even if they're not a massive star. I remember my very first pay cheque from football. I was in my first year of university in Belfast but had been playing for Distillery, an amateur team. They gave us about £6 for a match – the equivalent of about £75 today – as travel money. It was lovely getting an envelope after the game with money in it. Even if it was a modest sum, I was getting paid to play football, which was an incredible feeling.

In the October of 1971 Northern Ireland were playing an international game against the Soviet Union in Belfast, and some of the lads didn't turn up, so the manager Terry Neill brought me into the squad as a substitute. I was with the likes of Pat Rice, Sammy Nelson and Pat Jennings. I got on for the last 15 minutes of the game and I'm not sure I even got a kick. It raised my profile, though, and after that things moved quickly. A Nottingham Forest scout came to our house and said the club was going to offer £15,000. It got accepted and that was a really big fee for Distillery to receive, especially given the situation in Northern Ireland back then. It was a really difficult time for everyone, and Distillery were essentially broke. The money came in handy for them. So off I went to Nottingham.

I had no agent, but my older brother, Leo, helped with the transfer because I had to switch from amateur to professional. It was all straightforward compared to now. Given agents were uncommon back then, players probably lost out a bit financially. We probably could have got more money if we'd had an agent with us who was a better negotiator. At the time, none of that really mattered to me because I just wanted to play football in England. Money was not something I was thinking about. My first pay-cheque at Forest was for £45 per week, or around £560 in today's money, which is not a great deal more than the modern minimum wage. Forest were in the top division when

I joined, although we got relegated in my first season. The best player was Ian Storey-Moore, a top-quality winger, and he was earning about £150 a week, or about £1,800 in today's money. A similar player today – the best player for one of the Premier League's smaller teams – might be on £100,000 or £150,000 a week. The difference is vast. The club had the control then, which has been the key change. The shift has been enormous.

When I was offered a contract by Nottingham Forest, they said, 'This is the salary.' You went in to try to negotiate, but you didn't really know how to do that, compared to a professional agent. Sometimes you would have conversations about wages with a teammate you trusted, and for me that was John Robertson. I didn't really know what my other teammates earned in general. I did get paid more as we won trophies, and I have no complaints or regrets about money. When I look back on my playing career, money was very far down the list of the things I thought about then.

Money and Attitude

When I think about the way the attitudes of players have changed, sometimes nowadays they are quite resistant to things that would have seemed obvious in my day – like moving house when you get a job at the other end of the country and are required at training every morning. At Aston Villa we had a rule, as most clubs do, that players had to live locally, perhaps less than 25 miles from the training ground. Some of the lads would buy a little place in the town centre, but would hardly be there, and would in fact be commuting 100 miles or more, multiple times a week. Some would live around London, or in Cheshire, where the players of the Liverpool and Manchester clubs tend to live. It is understandable why people might want to stay where they are, if they have a wife or children and don't want to disrupt their lives, but they are certainly paid enough money to relocate comfortably. A long commute is no good for someone who wants to play sport at the very highest level.

At Villa I signed Steve Sidwell from Chelsea. He was at Reading for a long time before that, so lived down south, a fairly long way from the Villa training ground just north of Birmingham. I would see him getting out of his car after those two-and-a-half hour drives and he wanted to know why he had a sore back. After a while it really irritated me. I thought, if players are going to travel that far they could at least get a taxi. That much driving is no good for you as a player. Usually we would start training at 9.45 a.m., and if a player has done a drive like that he will be stiff as a poker. You would be irritated when those players went into the training complex and then jumped on a treatment table to get a massage, purely because of all the driving. You couldn't micromanage every aspect of their lives, though. Some things you could prove, and others you couldn't. A player might say they were in one location when they might be elsewhere, but you couldn't know for sure. You have to trust players to an extent. It all comes back to this thing of not being able to treat everyone the same. You never begrudge the top player pushing the boundaries a little bit if his attitude is otherwise good, and he's putting in the performances. It's the lesser player earning a lot of money that becomes an issue: you're allowed to do pretty much whatever you like if you're as good as Cristiano Ronaldo – but most aren't.

At Leicester I remember signing Robbie Savage from Crewe just after we'd been promoted to the Premier League. After signing the contract Robbie got himself an expensive car. I saw it parked outside the training ground. I didn't like the idea of a new signing publicly parading his newfound wealth. I had a quiet word with him and, in fairness to Robbie, he replaced the car. Nowadays salaries are often published the day after a signing in the newspapers. Agents often put it out there because it helps drive up wages for everyone, and they get a bigger cut too. The money players earn in the big leagues is just phenomenal now. Rolex watches and flash cars abound, and not just among the very top players, who you don't begrudge it as much, but also the ones who aren't necessarily that good.

The danger is that this wealth at the top level is just constantly spiralling upwards. What happens is that if you give one player a big contract, somebody else gets to know, and they ask for more as well. You always feel as if you are benchmarking against what the very top players earn, rather than comparing to ones of a similar level. Surely it must affect players too, if instead of focusing on the trophies they have won, they are constantly comparing their salaries to what their peers are earning.

One thing I feel sad about is that with all this new money coming in, I thought ticket prices would come down, making it easier for someone to take their family to the match. Logically that would make sense – the clubs are less reliant on ticket sales, which make up a far smaller percentage of annual revenue than used to be the case. But that didn't happen, and alongside tickets becoming more and more expensive, so did replica shirts and all the other things a child might want, as well as the cost of travelling around the country. The game has become far more remote from the man in the street. It is hard for people on ordinary incomes to afford tickets to games at the top level. It means the working-class element of the game, which has its roots in the factories and communities of England's north and Midlands, is disappearing. It is a great shame.

There is lots of money in the game but too much is distributed at the top. Nowadays when teams get promoted it feels like a phenomenal achievement to stay up, but the idea of winning titles feels remote for all but a handful of clubs. Clubs want more and more cash to pay the wages of players, be that through TV, ticket receipts, sponsorship deals or whatever else. Tickets are a relatively small amount of the money the top clubs own, and yet the prices are still astronomical. Football stadiums are increasingly becoming a place for wealthy people, rather than the working-class environments they were in my day. It is good that people are getting into football who weren't before, but this can dilute the atmosphere and culture when fans are priced out. Football has become a big-money industry.

An Unequal Game

The influx of money into the English game has not just benefited the likes of Manchester City and Chelsea. Teams like Wrexham and Birmingham City have received big backing; lower league English football has appealed to investors because buying into the Premier League is now so hard. I wonder what will happen with Wrexham, because if they get seriously high up the football pyramid it will get more and more expensive to compete – a seven-digit sum can go a long way lower down the leagues, but higher up an eight- or even nine-figure sum can barely touch the sides. It doesn't cost a huge sum of money to get promoted out of the National League, but becoming even a mid-table Premier League side is a massively expensive business. I think all this international investment is exciting, though. Personally speaking, if you're a multibillionaire and you want to buy a football club and you take a team from the third or fourth division then make them into the best team in the world, I generally think, 'Fine, go for it.' The English game is massive around the world now, and we should embrace that.

In comparison, Scottish football has fallen into financial decline. The likes of Fulham or Bournemouth now have far more money than Celtic or Rangers. There was a gap during my time in Glasgow but it has got far bigger since then. There is really very little money in Scottish football compared to in England. Celtic have had success and benefited from Champions League money, which could be £30 million, perhaps, in a good season, but that isn't much relatively speaking. The lowest Premier League teams get more than £100 million from TV revenue, let alone the biggest teams who get far more. In Scotland the domestic TV revenue is miniscule in comparison. It is a huge imbalance, although there's also a huge gulf between Celtic and Rangers and the smaller clubs in Scotland. There is little interest outside Scotland in the TV rights, so the money is small, whereas the Premier League is watched globally, and England has about ten times the population of Scotland, so that is a lot more TV subscriptions domestically. Scotland is a special place when it comes to football, though – per head of population, it has the highest match-going population in the whole of Europe.

Celtic and Rangers are huge institutions all over the world. If those two clubs were ever in the English league they would attract audiences like you wouldn't believe, far more than some of the clubs you see competing in the top flight these days. There has been some talk of it over the years but I don't think it's going to happen. There is simply no incentive for Premier League teams to give up two spaces like that, and the Premier League is a members' club where the clubs have to vote for any rule changes. It would be like turkeys voting for Christmas if you were a mid-table Premier League team, as relegation would suddenly become a lot more likely. About 20 years ago the Football League were interested in having Celtic and Rangers join, starting out at the very bottom. You can see why those lower English clubs would like it: every Celtic and Rangers game would get a full house, and it would attract lots of attention and money. The Premier League decided against it though. I understand why; I would oppose it if I was one of those clubs, but Scottish football is really being left behind, especially since Rangers were liquidated and reformed in 2012. They did win a league title in 2021 but, aside from that, Scotland began to feel like a one-team league at the time. Of course, I am biased towards Celtic, but the impact on Scottish football has not been good. It feels like the quality of non-Old Firm teams – Motherwell or Aberdeen, for example – has declined.

Perhaps one good thing about the crazy money at the top of the English game these days is that it gives players a financial safety net if things go wrong, in a career that peaks and ends at a very young age. Colin Barrett was an important player in the story of Nottingham Forest. He was a full-back between 1976 and 1980, making the journey with me from Division Two to the league title and European glory. He scored one of the most important goals in the club's history: the second in a 2–0 win against Liverpool in the first round of the European Cup in 1978–79. That really put the tie out of reach late in the game before we went to Anfield and ground out a 0–0. But just ten days after that first leg he suffered a terrible knee injury and listened to the return game from his hospital bed and barely played again. He was only 26 when it happened. Whenever he tried to come back, his knee gave way. Medicine was far less advanced, and many careers were ended by a bad tackle or just a bad stroke of luck. In the case of Colin Barrett, it meant that he never got the chance to negotiate a new contract as a player who had just won the European Cup, so he never earned that much as a footballer.

He ended up working at a pub just outside Nottingham for a bit, and then he became a self-employed painter and decorator for a long time, which was his second career. There's absolutely nothing wrong with any of that, but you can't imagine it now for a player who has reached those heights. The wages are so high today for any player getting anywhere near a European Cup that even if they had a career-ending injury they would be set up for life, so long as they invest their money wisely. Not only were wages so much lower back then but there were none of the massive sponsorship deals that would come along in later years. For the very top players these days, their sponsorship deals can be worth even more than their salary.

Bobby Moore is another good example of how huge the shift has been in how much the top players earn. Moore, of course, captained England to the World Cup in 1966, making him perhaps the greatest English footballer of all time. But a few years later he was a jobbing radio commentator. Harry Redknapp said that Moore once got kicked out of Upton Park during a match because he didn't have the right ticket, which is unbelievable. Moore couldn't get anywhere in club management, there were no lucrative sponsorship deals, so he needed to find radio work to pay the bills. Imagine the sponsorship deals today if you were an England captain who won the World Cup! It all feels very strange now, given that his name conjures up images of the greatest day in English football history, that image of him in the red shirt on his teammates' shoulders. Despite all that, Moore was a very modest man. Because he was the captain of a team that won the World Cup, and England have been striving to win it again ever since then, he is almost a bigger figure now than he was just after he retired, particularly given the fact he sadly died in 1993 at the age of just 51.

I was fortunate in the second half of my life because I earned some decent money as a manager and I was comfortable financially. I got that second opportunity, but some people I played with never did, and had to make drastic career changes that you would not associate with a professional footballer now. This was not because they've mismanaged their finances, but simply because they never earned very much.

Too Much too Young?

The finances involved when it comes to very young footballers are crazy now. Let's say you're 17 years old and a half decent player with a shot of making the grade at the top level. You might be earning £10,000 or £15,000 a week now, which is an extraordinary sum of money – more than all but the very top handful of bankers and lawyers working in the City. It is obvious that there will be a sense of entitlement that comes with that, at an age when you are not equipped to deal with it. Sometimes there is a big fight among several clubs to sign a young player and a parent or another relative is the agent. As a manager you might have to deal with the whole family, perhaps show them around and convince them that your club is better than the alternatives, which is a totally new thing.

Families are often very money-motivated, which is completely understandable from their perspective. If you are from a family without a lot of money, your child getting one big contract can set all of you up for life. I don't think this attitude always helps the player, though, and it is not even necessarily in the long-term financial interests of the family if the player makes the wrong move early in their career. As a young player it is usually better to be playing regularly for a 'smaller' club with a lower profile and maybe less money than not getting in the squad for a big-name team, where people might just forget about you, and your career can stall. I was recently speaking to an agent who is dealing with all this. He says there are players he has looked after since they were young children, and then they turn 17 and someone offers them crazy money and they snap it up. But the short-term financial boost might not benefit a player in the long run. Some clubs have players on the books that have never even been to the training ground, they are just constantly out on loan, almost like lines on a balance sheet rather than footballers. Does that give those individual players the best chance to consistently develop?

Players get signed up so much younger now as well. I was signed at 19 by Forest, which would be far too old now. These days you get six-year-olds being scouted by the top clubs. The schedule is so intense, with their parents having to drive around all over the place and maybe sacrifice work or other things, and there is every likelihood that a child that young won't make it at the top level. It might even make them worse players, because their natural abilities can be coached out of them so quickly. For the vast majority that don't make it, they may well have spent those years in academies not pursuing their education properly, so will have fewer opportunities outside the game when it chews them up and spits them out, as happens more often than not.

While thinking about how money has changed football over the years, I dug out a document from my days at Leicester City back in 1996 when the board members were considering floating the club on the stock market shortly after getting promoted to the Premier League. It is a fascinating read. Even though it was not that long ago, there was just so much less money sloshing around compared to today. This was just before English football exploded after Euro '96 and the big TV deals came along, even though the Premier League was well underway. The document says football turnover increased from £1.5 million to £5.8 million between 1991 and 1995 due to 'improved football performance'; factoring in commercial turnover it was closer to £10 million. That is peanuts in today's game, even when you think about inflation. The least successful teams in the Premier League now make more than £100 million a year, before you even get on to ticket revenue and commercial income, and the biggest ones make many times that.

When it comes to spending, the biggest difference between then and now is wages. The Leicester document shows that our best-paid player was on £104,000 a year, or £2,000 a week, which is worth roughly double that in today's money when you account for inflation, so far less than the equivalent would be earning now. Of course to most people that would be a brilliant wage, but not in football these days. It would be a typical wage some way down the pyramid, not a star player for a team getting promoted to the Premier League.

When it comes to that Leicester document, a lot of the less well-known players on the list – not star players but squad players – were on £41,000 a year, which again would be worth double that in today's money accounting for inflation. That is absolutely peanuts in the modern game. There might have been some bonuses but, overall, there was just far less money. Remember this isn't ancient history, it was 1996, four years after the Premier League came into existence. It took a few years before things really took off after that 1997 TV deal. Looking through that document makes Leicester City look like a small regional business rather than a company operating at the international level it is today, even if the club is far behind many others in England in that sense.

Sponsorship

As well as more money coming in from TV, the level of sponsorship is incredible now. Manchester United have underperformed for more than a decade but, in 2023, Adidas agreed to pay a minimum of £900 million to make their kits over ten years. The level of cash is staggering because now these clubs are global brands rather than just domestic ones. When I won the European Cup at Nottingham Forest our kits weren't sponsored at all. The shirts were made by Adidas, all red with three white stripes on the sleeve, but there was no sponsor logo on the front. That could have been a good billboard for a company on the front page of every newspaper that day, and for the rest of history, but shirt sponsorship deals didn't become widespread until a few years later. Liverpool were the first big English side to get their shirt sponsored – by Hitachi, a Japanese electronics company, in the summer of 1979, between our two European Cups. Forest didn't get one until 1981, which was just after the glory years. That was with Panasonic, another Japanese electronics company. There were a lot of them back then, like JVC at Arsenal and Sharp at Manchester United. The shirts have changed a lot too. Now they are high-tech and a light fabric, but back in my day they were cotton and would get heavy in the rain. I particularly remember the one I wore at Norwich City, which was made of material that just stuck to you. The rise in replica shirts worn by fans of all ages as fashion marks another big change. I went to an Arsenal game not so long ago – it was a sunny day, and as I was walking in alongside lots of supporters it struck me how many of them were wearing shirts, both young kids wearing the latest one, and older people wearing a Tony Adams shirt. It wasn't a big thing for fans to wear the replica kits like they do now, perhaps for children, but not adults. Now every team has a big shirt sponsorship deal, and you will see the logos on fans of all ages walking about in the street as well as players on the pitch.

When it comes to sponsors, Barcelona were notable for not having one for a long time, but the financial pressures became too great and they were sponsored by Qatar Airways, then Spotify, after a deal with the charity UNICEF who Barcelona actually paid to be on their shirts. It is hard to imagine that now. At Aston Villa we let a local children's hospital, Acorns, have their logo on our shirts for free, but it's less feasible to do that now because the money pressures are so great. It's not just at the top of the game; far down the pyramid, sponsorship deals will be vital to clubs. There are deals for individuals as well as clubs now, and players all have their own sponsorship deals for boots, as well as advertising products. I used to sometimes pay for my own boots, even when I was winning European Cups and playing at the World Cup. The club might have given you one pair of studded boots, and a separate pair for if it was icy, and you might be given one more pair during the course of the year, but after that you would have to buy your own. Compare that to today's razzmatazz around football boots. When Adidas launched their new Predator boot in January 2025 there was a massive global social media campaign featuring Zinedine Zidane and Jude Bellingham, who I'm pretty sure doesn't have to buy his own boots.

In my playing days you could happily have gone through your whole career fairly oblivious to things like sponsorship and revenue streams, but there is much more awareness now. As a manager I was always happy in principle for the club to be making more money in this way, because it meant more to spend on transfer fees and wages, which, of course, helped you win football matches. Sometimes the priorities could feel wrong, though. At Aston Villa, the day after we reached the League Cup final by beating Blackburn Rovers 6–4 at Villa Park, the owner Randy Lerner held a big dinner for all the heads of departments. That was when I realised that I was just a head of a department, alongside the lady who was brilliant at running the restaurant. She had loads and loads of tables, and everything was going great. There were other employees there too who were very good at their jobs – and I don't want to disrespect what they were doing in any way – but I thought the whole thing showed a fundamental misunderstanding of how football works. I said to Randy, 'I don't want to say this to you, but everything comes back to the team winning football matches. The restaurant will not be full if the team is losing.' Eventually, they had to close the restaurant when the team got relegated a few years later. A football club is a big business with lots of staff doing important things that aren't directly related to results on the pitch – but those results affect everything. The mood of everyone is completely different depending on whether you have just won two in a row or lost two in a row. It affects sponsorship, tickets, hospitality . . . everything. Being at a winning football club is the best feeling in the world – but being at a losing one can be toxic.

That's the thing about money and football. You get people coming into the game who treat it solely like a business, something to profit from; or treat players like assets on a balance sheet rather than humans who might score goals for you, or stop them at the other end. But football is different from any other business because what matters most is not making money but winning or losing football matches. Although so much has changed, that was true in the early 1970s when I started out, and it's true today.

5

DEFENDING

The world of tactics has certainly changed a lot since my playing days. For a start, people simply talk about tactics far more. In the era of Brian Clough, and Sir Alex Ferguson too, what we talked about was their man-management skills and their eye for a transfer that could really improve a team, not their tactical set-ups. When thinking about tactics and how they have changed over time, we can split matters into two categories: defensive tactics and attacking tactics. Your tactics are perhaps even more important defensively because, ultimately, if you've got very good players going forward, you are likely to score goals. But in defence there is more importance attached to your shape, your style of play, and things like defending set-pieces and offside traps, which take a bit of thought.

Two noteworthy defensive performances when managing the Republic of Ireland come to mind. Both games, one in Gelsenkirchen, the other in Dublin, against the reigning World Champions, Germany, had similar traits, but the four points we took from those two games essentially paved the way for us to qualify for the 2016 European Championships, the last time the Republic of Ireland qualified for a major competition. Massive underdogs against such a formidable force, our plan of containment worked for such a long period in the away game, with players tracking back at the least sign of danger, closing the opposition down quickly when they had sight of goal. Even when we were breached with a Tony Kroos goal with about 15 minutes left, we showed amazing fighting spirit which culminated in John O'Shea snatching a last-minute equaliser and sending our travelling fans into delirium.

Amazingly, in the return match in Dublin in October 2015, we went one better. Again the World Champions dominated possession but, football being football, goals didn't necessarily follow. Our defensive display in Gelsenkirchen months earlier gave us the belief that we could thwart their attacks, but find room to attack them also when opportunities arose. And that it did when Shane Long drove home a magnificent goal to topple this star-studded German team. In fact, their starting line-up contained seven World Cup winners, while Championship players abounded in our team. On the night, they played like superstars and their performance not only endeared them to the supporters in the stadium but to the whole country watching on. Shane Long's goal is still a topic of conversation today.

And in the Euros in France in 2016 the team excelled defensively once again, against Italy in the northern town of Lille. This time victory was an absolute must if we were to progress to the last 16 of the competition, so while having to stay resilient defensively, we had to find a way to attack, even from deep positions. And with only minutes left, with the game goalless primarily because of our players' never-say-die attitude, Robbie Brady etched his name into Republic of Ireland football folklore by courageously heading a wonder goal to win the game. A heroic performance against one of the favourites for the competition itself does make you glow with immense pride and satisfaction.

Different Opponents, Different Tactics

So from a tactical viewpoint, plans and counter plans were formulated according to the opposition, mindful of course that our opponents would also have plans of their own. But never underestimate the fighting spirit and the will to win that can win football matches when those carefully thought-out plans do not seem to be working.

When dealing with those international opponents, naturally, different tactics would be used, depending on the opposition and also whether the game was at home or away.

Home advantage, more often than not, forces you on to the offensive from the early stages of a game. There is nothing wrong with that at all but, as was the case with Germany in Dublin when they dominated possession, we found ourselves on the back foot from almost the first minute simply because they had world class players at their disposal. But in that group we were up against Scotland, Poland and Georgia, all tough games for us, and also Gibraltar that we would be expected to beat, both home and away.

Those Scotland and Poland games were tough. We drew at home and lost away against both, which was disappointing. Those four points against the Germans, though, were enough to send us through to a two-legged play-off against Bosnia and Herzegovina. The first leg was away in the city of Zenica. It was a tough old match and very foggy. We didn't have much possession but Robbie Brady scored late on and we thought we had clinched a famous win – then Edin Džeko, a Premier League winner with Manchester City of course, pegged us back. It still gave us a great chance back in Dublin, and we won 2–0 with Jon Walters scoring two penalties. In the dressing room afterwards there were wild scenes of euphoria because we had qualified for France and we knew we would have a huge travelling contingent, like Jack Charlton's Ireland side did in the USA in 1994. The Irish fans seem to be welcomed wherever they go and are almost always in good spirits, which you can't say for every country's fans.

In the lead-up to the tournament we stayed in a comfortable hotel near Versailles outside Paris, and we were training every day for two weeks. It was like being with a club side in that respect, a feeling you don't often get as a national team manager. At the tournament itself, as well as beating Italy we got a good 1–1 draw against a Swedish side including Zlatan Ibrahimović, before being well beaten 3–0 by a very strong Belgian team. We went through to the knockouts and were unlucky to be drawn against France, who were the strong favourites for the tournament on home soil. We had an incredible start with a penalty in the second minute to make it 1–0 but we just couldn't hold them off and Antoine Griezmann scored twice to make it 2–1. It was a heroic effort, but still disappointing – you never feel good after losing a football match, even when you've played well against a top team.

In games like that one against France, I had to think about my tactical set-up very carefully because we were the big underdogs, and ultimately you have to accept that the opponent has stronger players. If you try to go toe-to-toe with them you will lose. You know you are going to have less possession. You're going to have to try to play as tightly and as strongly as possible, certainly in the early stages. You want to frustrate the opposition and run down the clock, but if you can quell them for the first 15 minutes, things get a little easier and you start to grow more confident that you can achieve something. You're relying on your players not making mistakes, not diving or giving away a penalty or leaving big gaps at the back. But you have to take a bit of a risk at times if you want to score a goal. You can't just sit back for 90 minutes. You have to give players licence to leave their defensive job sometimes, because if you don't even try to score you are almost certain to lose – it's extremely hard to keep a clean sheet against the best attackers in the world. You always feel that the best players can break you down eventually, so there have to be calculated risks alongside strong defensive play. Mental fatigue plays a role as well. Just like physical fatigue, it's exhausting when you're under the pump like that for 90 minutes, far more so than when you're dominating the ball in a game. You feel completely different at the end of the 90 minutes depending on whether you've spent the whole time with your backs against the wall or not.

The most important thing for me in those games against the likes of Germany, Italy and France was to get players who were used to playing at a far lower level to believe that they could compete for 90 minutes against the best in the world. If I didn't achieve that we would have lost before we started. The psychology is really important. I would tell the team, 'While these opposing players are very good, you can compete with them and take the ball off them if you are mentally alert for the whole game. If you make a mistake your teammate will help you out in the same way you will help them. If you are still in the game after 50 or 60 minutes the mental and physical fatigue will not set in in the same way as it will if you are losing.' Once you start chasing a game, you get more tired and open yourself up to conceding more goals, and your opponent might just start passing it around at the back, which is exhausting if you are behind.

Another excellent defensive performance that sticks in my memory occurred in the League Cup final in 1996–97, Leicester City's first season back in the Premier League. My tactical tweak was key to winning only the second major trophy in the club's history, following a League Cup win in 1964. We were big underdogs in the final against Middlesbrough, who had finished mid-table in the Premier League the season before. They had the Brazilian player Juninho, who was probably the best attacking midfielder in the Premier League at the time. Alongside him there were two other brilliant attackers who started that final: Emerson, another Brazilian, and the Italian striker Fabrizio Ravanelli. Juninho was the one to watch though. Two weeks before the final we'd hosted them at Filbert Street and he destroyed us pretty much on his own. They went 3–0 up after 36 minutes. We got one back but Juninho ran rings around us that day. I couldn't allow that to happen again so decided that we would man-mark Juninho in the final. I gave the job to a Swedish defender called Pontus Kåmark who I knew would have the discipline to do it, even though he had never done this job before. It worked. We kept Juninho quiet and the game ended 0–0 after 90 minutes before going to extra-time. Ravanelli scored early on but then Emile Heskey equalised in the last minute.

That was the last ever year that the League Cup final went to a replay if it ended a draw, and two weeks later we played again at Hillsborough in Sheffield. We adopted the same approach towards Juninho in the replay, and it finished 0–0 again after 90 minutes before our striker Steve Claridge scored the only goal in extra-time and I lifted my first top-level trophy. It was an amazing feeling and the victory was down to those tactics, because Kåmark barely allowed Juninho a kick over the two games, which was the main reason we won. That sort of man-marking is not very common, though. You can only justify it when there is one outstanding player on the opposition, because it means your team will inevitably get stretched elsewhere. If a team has three or four outstanding attacking players such tactics are not really going to work because they can just pull you all over the place. But in those games by keeping Juninho quiet we kept the whole team from creating much. Defensively, it is hard for the players who are not man-marking because they are having to move around constantly and be very aware of opposing players' movement and where their teammates are. One lapse in concentration and it can all go badly wrong, but over those two games we executed it to perfection.

Player Roles

When I look back and consider how defensive tactics have evolved over the years, what comes to mind is how various roles on the pitch have changed. One example that springs to mind relates to the Arsenal team managed by George Graham in the 1990s, who were known as 'boring, boring Arsenal' because they were solid at the back and not so thrilling to watch. But they were very effective defensively, in part because of a significant tactical change that is barely remarked upon now. Before that side, most teams had their full-backs play the offside line – acting as the last defenders before the goalkeeper, stepping up and trying to play an opponent offside. Arsenal tried something innovative. They had their two centre-halves – Steve Bould and

Tony Adams – play the offside line, with the full-backs pushing higher up the pitch. This enabled the full-backs to be more attacking. When Bould and Adams put their arms in the air to indicate their opponent was offside they shouted so vociferously and loudly that the linesman usually gave it. I'm sure lots of the time it wasn't actually offside, but there was no VAR back then. Arsenal had the offside trap down to a tee under Graham, who was the absolute master of defensive tactics, and it worked very well for them. Watching from a distance, I could see that this worked better than using the full-backs because the centre-halves were closer together, so they could hear each other and see and hear the signals. The two full-backs were naturally further up the pitch so you didn't need to worry about them in terms of playing someone onside. In the English game of the early 1990s, that was an Arsenal innovation, but these days it's completely standard that the centre-halves play the offside line.

A decade or so later José Mourinho brought a whole new defensive philosophy to the Premier League. He was all about closing up shop and winning matches and trophies, and was very successful in that, as I unfortunately know too well. If you watch back the 2003 UEFA Cup final, which my Celtic team lost to his Porto, their goalkeeper Vítor Baía kept going down in the last six or seven minutes, lying there for ages and killing off the game. This was before the recent change where referees add far more injury time if teams run down the clock, so it was really effective in killing things off after they had gone 3–2 up in extra-time. John Terry, who was Chelsea's captain and best defender throughout his time there, said Mourinho told him that if Chelsea were defending with a couple of minutes to go, two players should hit the floor when the ball came in because the referee would immediately stop the game, taking the steam out of things a bit. This style of play isn't attractive to watch but it wins you trophies, and Terry and Mourinho won a lot of them. Mourinho has been a really great manager, in England and elsewhere. Inter Milan's Champions League semi-final win over Barcelona in 2010 was a masterclass in ultra-defensive tactics, and they went on to lift the trophy.

Elsewhere on the pitch, there has been a huge evolution in the role of the goalkeeper. Keepers in my day were primarily tasked with stopping the ball from going into the net, and that was pretty much it. They didn't have to worry about being good with their feet because, as I explained in chapter 3, the back-pass rule didn't exist. A keeper could pick the ball up if he got into trouble, wait a while, then kick it down the field. As well as the back-pass rule, another reason goalkeeping has had to evolve tactically is because of pressing – teams running hard at the opposition to try to get the ball back quickly. The level of pressing has increased hugely over the past decade or so as teams have reached new levels of fitness. Klopp's Liverpool were really good at constantly putting the keeper under pressure in this way, with players like Mohamed Salah, Roberto Firmino and Sadio Mané running and running all game. Keepers have to be better with their feet because they have less time on the ball. The more confident a keeper is in his footwork, the better he will be able to deal with players coming at him. In the seventies and eighties there would be times when the ball would be in the opposition half and the keeper would almost have time for a snooze – if you won a game comfortably the goalkeeper often barely touched the ball. That's another big tactical change – keepers today are much more involved in the build-up play.

I was lucky to have played in front of two of the best keepers: Pat Jennings on the international stage and Peter Shilton for a number of years at Forest. Shilton was a brilliant shot stopper, which is the main thing you want in the keeper as a teammate. If Shilton played these days he might struggle because he wasn't so good with his feet, but that doesn't stop him from being one of the best goalkeepers that has ever played the game. If there's one criticism I'd have regarding goalkeepers playing with their feet now, it would be that footwork has taken precedence over the basic task of stopping shots, which has to always be the main priority. I cynically believe that goalkeepers do not see things how an outfield player does, and sometimes they end up getting themselves into sticky situations by keeping hold of the ball too long. I get nervous when I see them getting closed down when they play it short. Managers often insist on playing out from the back now, but I am not convinced it is always the best tactic.

Pat Jennings maybe had the edge on Shilton in the air, but Shilton was very agile and really put the hours into practising. This was in the era preceding goalkeeping coaches, which had become standard by the time I was a top-level manager. With goalkeepers, you have to delegate aspects of their coaching because it's a specialist position. I once had an interview at Stoke City and was offered the job but ended up not taking it, in part because they asked me if I would keep the goalkeeping coach on and I thought that should be my own decision. With goalkeepers there can be a sort of a cosiness attached to the role because they spend all day with such a small group, isolated from the rest of the squad. Outfield players, on the other hand, practise together, with attackers going up against defenders and suchlike, meaning they mix with far more people in an average day of training. Goalkeepers form this tight relationship with the goalkeeping coach and feel as if the coach should be standing up for them all the time.

The keeper is also an unusual position in that there is an inherent competition there. In other parts of the pitch there might be a way of getting two good players into the team, but that's obviously not going to happen with the goalkeeper, which can make it a difficult position to manage. When I arrived at Aston Villa I signed Scott Carson on loan from Liverpool, who did a good job for me in the 2007–08 season. That man has lived the life of Riley. He won the Champions League with Liverpool in 2005, then won it again with Man City 18 years later as their third-choice keeper. He almost never played for those two giants, but got to spend time with some of the world's best players and go on open-top bus parades. Lucky him, although to be fair he did have a long and distinguished career, playing hundreds of games for clubs including Aston Villa as well as

West Bromwich Albion, Wigan Athletic, Derby County and Bursaspor in Turkey.

I was always a bit wary of players who were happy to not play, but it can be quite useful with goalkeepers – you can never keep two keepers happy if they want to play every game. I had a goalkeeper at Leicester City called Pegguy Arphexad who didn't play much so went to Liverpool as their back-up. He was only there for three seasons and he won six medals – the same number of games he played! I could never understand a reserve goalkeeper being happy about that situation in the long-term, though. Sometimes for an easy life you don't mind a goalkeeper that's happy enough to be there and put up with the situation, but I don't like to see really good goalkeepers not playing games for long periods of time.

As I've said, because of the changes to the back-pass rule, young goalkeepers now learn to play the ball on the floor as much as they learn shot stopping. People think that all started with Pep Guardiola but it goes back longer than that. Things were already changing during my time at Aston Villa in the late 2000s. I remember two Manchester United goalkeepers, Fabien Barthez and Edwin van der Sar, as being particularly good with their feet. But the big change came when Pep Guardiola joined Manchester City in 2016 and got rid of Joe Hart, who he saw as not being good enough with his feet, replacing him with Claudio Bravo and Willy Caballero at first, then Ederson in the long term. It was harsh on Hart because he was an extremely good goalkeeper. He won lots of trophies with Celtic after people thought his career was finished. It clearly worked for Guardiola, because his teams went on to dominate English football for a decade.

Philosophy Versus Pragmatism

The physical intensity of the Premier League is so much higher now, with players often harrying their opponents relentlessly – pressing – to get the ball back. That is not the only way to defend, though. Sitting back and playing on the counter-attack can be effective too. Nottingham Forest demonstrated this brilliantly in the 2024–25 season, when they qualified for European football after nearly getting relegated the year before. In February 2025 they beat Brighton 7–0 with only 37 per cent possession, often defending by letting the other team simply have the ball. A few weeks earlier they had secured an excellent 1–1 draw with Liverpool with just 29 per cent of the ball in what amounted to a tactical masterclass: Liverpool hogged the ball but didn't create many clear-cut chances. Forest defended well all season and were lethal on the break with players like Morgan Gibbs-White, Anthony Elanga and Callum Hudson-Odoi, with Chris Wood getting on the end of chances. That same season I watched quite a bit of Spanish football and it often gets ugly because players try to hold on to the ball for too long and get pushed into corners. It's like they're all trying to be like that amazing Barcelona team of the 2010s but don't have the players to do it.

Those tactics worked brilliantly for Manchester City for a long time, but in the 2024–25 season you saw them struggle too. There isn't one good way to play. It depends on the circumstance and the players at your disposal. I sometimes think people are overly obsessed with styles and philosophies these days. I always preferred to be more pragmatic and adapt to the players I had, rather than insist on them playing a certain way. Vincent Kompany is a case in point. In his first season managing Burnley the team played lovely football and blew everyone away in the Championship to get promoted to the Premier League. When they reached the Premier League they tried the same tactic but lost pretty much every week and got relegated. If I had been the owner of Burnley, I might have been saying to Kompany, 'You did wonderfully well getting us up, but I want to try to keep my money – would you try to kick it just occasionally rather than all this playing out from the back?' Kompany landed on his feet though and ended up managing Bayern Munich! It was a major surprise when Xabi Alonso's Bayer Leverkusen won the Bundesliga in Kompany's first season at Bayern, because you expect Bayern to win every season given they hold almost all the cards financially. Kompany did do well to win in his second season, though, with Harry Kane winning a trophy after a long wait.

Great Defenders

When I think back to great defenders I played with, our Nottingham Forest team that won those European Cups had two centre-backs who were strong in the air: Kenny Burns and Larry Lloyd. Those two formed a really good partnership. In a Brian Clough side the main job of defenders was to defend. Anything else was a bonus. Viv Anderson at right-back would come forward a lot, but Clough would always say that his first job was to stop the ball coming in from out wide. Today full-backs come forward a lot more. It sometimes frustrates me when you see players nowadays who might be very good when attacking but seem incapable of stopping crosses coming in – they don't get tight and they back off the winger. That would have been anathema to Brian Clough.

Viv Anderson's job as right-back was to get out, engage a player and get within a yard of him, which he was very good at. He would try to slow things down so he wouldn't get beaten. Opposition full-backs would try to do the same to me as a winger, engaging me and sending me down the touchline away from the goal. If they succeeded, it would buy the centre-halves some time to recover and get in position, meaning that if I did get the ball in they could defend it. Brian Clough very much believed in showing the wingers down the line. His thinking was to keep the attacker as far away from the goal as possible so that if he did eventually beat his man, the centre-backs could deal with it. Terry Venables, who managed Tottenham, Barcelona and England, had a different view of things. He liked his full-backs to show players inside. His view was that he had other players inside who could deal with it and block them off. The big danger is if those players are not there to deal with it, you are in more trouble than if you get beaten out wide. A tactical change recently has seen the increase in 'inverted' players: a right-footed lad playing on the left-wing, say, who sees his job as cutting inside and trying to shoot, or wanting to play someone in centrally, rather than crossing from out wide. England have done that a lot in recent times with Marcus Rashford, who is right-footed, on the left, and Bukayo Saka, who is left-footed, on the right. Nowadays you see both styles, and full-backs have to be able to deal with both.

Another thing Clough was big on saying to his defenders was that they should know who they were playing against every week, even back when it was far harder to get footage to show to players, let alone detailed stats or data. He would say the forward should know what a defender would do in various situations, and that a defender should know which way a forward was going to go. The full-back's job in the 1970s was simpler in general because it was more of a straightforward defensive role, although there were exceptions. Terry Cooper at Leeds United was particularly keen to attack, but that was not his main job – that was to defend. As a winger I would always be having one-on-one tussles with the full-backs, and they would be trying to stop me and sending me away from the goal as much as possible, while I was trying to get it in the box, or drift in at the back post where hopefully I would get on the end of a John Robertson cross.

One thing that frustrates me today as part of this obsession with keeping the ball, even when you're pegged back in your own half, is when players make passes which land their teammates in trouble. I don't mean attacking passes such as trying to get the ball into a striker. Of course passes like that aren't going to come off every time, and you have to take risks or you will never score a goal. I'm talking about when a defender, say, has the ball deep in his own half and is playing to a forward teammate who is marked, but could lose possession. The defender races forward expecting the ball again, but it might not be as easy as that. The player who received the ball might get a chance to play it back to the goalkeeper, but maybe not if the attacker is hounding him. Brian Clough would have been furious about that, saying the defender who played the first ball had run away from the situation. It would have amounted to 'a dereliction of duty', he'd say, but it happens all the time in the modern game. It's the first thing that the older managers would have pulled you up on, getting forward too quickly when, in fact, 'all you've done', to quote Brian Clough, 'is put your mate in the shit'.

On one occasion we were training round the back of the City Ground. It was a very primitive place for a top-flight club to be training compared to what you see now. In Clough's early days at the club we played five-a-side or seven-a-side with the team that was going to be playing on Saturday. I remember one moment so well. I played a ball into the centre-forward but he was surrounded by two people. I ran round the corner asking him to make a pass that was really difficult for him to play. I thought I was doing a bit of movement, showing energy, doing the right thing. But Clough stopped the game immediately: 'What are you doing?!' I said I was playing it to get a one-two, but he was incredulous. 'A "one-two"? You play it into the centre-forward, he's marked, there's two men surrounding him, and you're playing a "one-two"?! Pelé couldn't have played that ball!' I'll always remember that; it had a big impact on me. He was right.

For all that Brian Clough taught me about football, he was not big on tactics as we know them today. There's a video clip from a documentary where he walks into a room with a tactics board and magnets and whatever else, and he looks at it and then turns to the camera and says, 'That's what's wrong with the game.' It's not hard to guess what he would think about the obsession with data and statistics in football today, especially the idea of 'expected goals', which I am very sceptical of myself. For a complicated man, Brian Clough preached simplicity, and I absolutely agree that football is still a simple game. Of course, I am behind the curve now. I would never get a job if I said all that in an interview.

Whether you can defend well or badly, keep a clean sheet or not, football is really all about players. In most cases, the best players will probably decide the game, no matter how brilliant or terrible the two teams' tactics. But that doesn't happen every time, and a tactical plan can be the difference in some games, and help a team win even if they might seem on paper to have lesser players. You always have to be aware, though, that just because you have a plan it doesn't mean it will work – and your opponent can always surprise you with something, meaning you will have to change things up. That's what I find strange about modern tactics sometimes: coaches often have this big overarching philosophy, and if they go a goal down or a goal up in the first minute, they won't change it. Maybe that works if you're Manchester City at the peak of your powers, but I think a lot of times it doesn't, and it comes across as stubborn while making it easy for the opposition to figure you out. With Clough it wasn't about tactics as such. He was so brilliant because he was a great man-manager. That's still what matters most of all. For all Guardiola's tactical brilliance, he has said himself that the main part of the job is still man-management. Klopp, too, was brilliant because he got inside players' heads, as did Sir Alex Ferguson.

After the game you might go over some of the tactics: what worked and what didn't. When it came to talking this through, a lot would depend on the result. If you'd won and played well, it was very easy in the dressing room. There wasn't much to say – 'Well done, have a nice evening. See you in a couple of days.' If you'd lost and played badly it was also easy to know what to say – not good things. The tricky one for a manager comes if the result is undeserved. Sometimes you win while playing badly. It's always easier for players to accept criticism when you've got the result. Also, as a manager you will be less strident in your criticism, because it's hard to be too angry about things if you've got the win, even if deep down you know you didn't really deserve it. The criticism feels more like constructive criticism than having a go at players when the mood is low, which can land badly. One of the most difficult situations to address is when you've played well and lost the game. I'm sure managers all say the same thing; I certainly have many times: 'Don't worry, if we keep playing like that we'll get a result.' The thing is, you might play well for the next three games and lose them all. Football is a low-scoring game and it is very common for the 'better' team to lose. If you lose three games in a row then it is a sign that things are really not all fine, even if you can pick lots of positives out of the performances.

Something that has definitely changed over time is the extent to which managers criticise players. I don't think players can take it to the same extent that they used to. This has certainly evolved during my time in management, and I imagine it continues to do so. I'd love to be in the dressing room with a team today and see how 'criticism' plays out. I never liked criticising or being angry for the sake of it, but if something wasn't good enough you needed to be able to say so firmly so you could fix it – that benefits everyone.

What Not to Do

As well as looking at some of the best defensive performances throughout football history, it can be instructive to look at some terrible ones. There has never been, even when the Champions League was called the European Cup, a more one-sided final than Paris Saint-Germain's demolition of Italian giants Inter Milan in Munich on the last day of May in 2025. While Paris rejoiced in sublime jubilation, the blue-and-black of Milan were stunned by such an abject performance from their team. Inter Milan, proud winners of this competition in the past, succumbed so meekly.

PSG showed character and resilience and rose gloriously to the occasion by obliterating Inter to win Europe's most coveted trophy. It seemed obvious they would want to dominate possession, and Inter would surely have made a plan to counteract this. Unfortunately for them they made no attempt throughout the game to prevent this happening, even though they were not outnumbered in the middle of the park. If someone had told me in mid-November of the previous year that a midfield trio of Fabián Ruiz, a youngster João Neves and Vitinha, who had not exactly pulled up any trees in a loan spell at Wolves a few seasons earlier, would boss a Champions League final for the entirety of the game, I would not have believed it possible, regardless of the opposition.

After all, Neymar himself said signing the likes of Vitinha had considerably weakened the PSG squad of which he was part.

Great player Neymar, but maybe not a great judge of players! As for Inter, Henrikh Mkhitaryan, at 36 years old, had seen better days. He laboured throughout his time on the field, unable to close players down, and then was unable to do anything with the ball on the very few occasions he was actually in possession. Years ago, I played with a brilliant Scottish midfield player called Asa Hartford. After one particular game in which he struggled – unusual for him – he said, self-mockingly: 'Today, I was everywhere the ball had just been.' We midfield players have all been there at times. Mkhitaryan and his two midfield colleagues, Hakan Çalhanoğlu and Nicolò Barella, could easily have coined that phrase themselves. At no stage could they get remotely close to the PSG midfield trio, who gleefully exploited the expansive room they were given.

Inter's wing-backs had very difficult evenings. Denzel Dumfries was a shadow of the player who had performed so well against Barcelona in both semi-finals. Federico Dimarco, on the left-hand side, had a torrid time before being substituted. He has a cultured left foot when on the ball but a total inability to defend one-on-one situations, with hands behind his back, not closing down the space and not being in a position to adjust his feet to deal with an oncoming attacker.

When teams play with three at the back, defenders rely heavily on wing-backs to help them out, sometimes wanting them to do the job they are supposed to be doing themselves. Dimarco found himself not only defending deeply, but unsure of which player to go and mark when PSG moved the ball quickly from their left to their right. The Inter wing-back looked completely bewildered in his own penalty area, thus playing PSG onside for the first goal and not closing the ball down properly for the second – and fatal – goal. Dimarco rarely received any help from Mkhitaryan. Alessandro Bastoni, rated by good judges as one of the best defenders in Europe, was also poor.

It was a sorry mess of a display that had listlessness written all over it. The constant inability to play out from the back, despite repeated attempts to do so, must have been an irritation to the Inter supporters, those within the stadium and those watching on TV in Italy. I do not recall one occasion when they broke the PSG press. More often than not they played themselves into trouble in doing so.

PSG, alert to what Inter were going to do, were like sprinters coiled on their blocks anticipating the starter's gun; they rushed Inter so quickly and so effectively that Yann Sommer in the Inter goal ended up kicking the ball long, awkwardly, sometimes into touch. No player likes to be exposed, particularly defenders when faced up against good attackers. Inter players were chasing shadows all evening. Indeed, in boxing parlance, Inter never laid a glove on PSG the whole match. They have much to regret.

My Tactics

People sometimes ask what my tactics were as a manager. That's a difficult question to answer, because they changed over time. Lots of managers today seem to have a fixed tactical philosophy and try to fit their players into that but, as I've been saying, I was always a firm believer in fitting the system to the players. At Leicester I usually played three at the back, a 3–5–2 formation with wing-backs who I liked to be forward-thinking players. This wasn't through any philosophy but was due to the players I had when I arrived at Leicester. Steve Walsh was the main centre-half, and I had lots of others who could play alongside him but who I thought would have been incapable of playing in a back four. It would have been too brittle – you need to be a really good defender to play in a back four as one of just two centre-halves. With three there is more cover, and the two wing-backs can track back to make it a five if need be.

Over time at Leicester I signed some better defenders, in Gerry Taggart, and Matty Elliott, who went on to play 199 times in the Premier League for Leicester, as well as winning the League Cup twice with me. He was big and strong but could really play the ball, which is a hugely valuable attribute in a defender. I signed another defender, Frank Sinclair, for another reason: he was very quick. He could read a situation and get back to help if needed. I also loved managing Neil Lennon, a midfielder and a huge part of our defensive game at both Leicester and Celtic. He was Celtic's equivalent of Roy Keane, the driving force in midfield, and he later won a lot of trophies as Celtic manager.

Over time three centre-halves became part of my set-up, which I continued with when I went to Celtic. Like all systems, it is fallible, particularly if you have centre-halves who don't really want to come out to wider positions. One occasion it went wrong was the time we lost 3–0 to Porto in 2001, two years before we lost more narrowly to the same side in the UEFA Cup final. That game taught me a lesson about setting up with three at the back. We had played so well against Ajax, who were probably just as good a side as Porto. We beat them in the qualifying round, including a 3–1 win in Amsterdam which was fantastic. But then it was almost as if Porto had seen that and come up with a plan to beat us by pushing up three attackers on to our three centre-backs. I hadn't experienced this sort of thing too often in Scotland, because it requires committing a lot of bodies forward, and we were usually dominating games domestically (although Rangers did it once or twice to us to good effect).

Porto essentially had two wide players as well as the centre-forward pushing up on my three centre-halves, really condensing the game in such a manner that the rest of the players barely got a look-in. Our wing-backs Alan Thompson and Didier Agathe, who were forward-thinking players, were not getting back into position to defend. It essentially meant we were three-on-three sometimes, and then an extra player, Deco, would come in from midfield. We conceded a goal in the first minute and another just before half-time. We were completely overrun. I didn't like to change my tactics early in games, but you have to be pragmatic, and on that occasion it was essential. I took off Thompson for midfielder Ľubomír Moravčík and went into a back four. It was far too late in that game, but it taught me a valuable lesson. Deco was absolutely brilliant and went on to be a key part of the Porto side that won the UEFA Cup and Champions League. Those are the types of things that you realise in the game. You always have a plan, but you have to remember the other team has a plan too.

Generally speaking, if you have a centre-half playing in a three, he doesn't really want to go out wide. That's not his nature; his nature is to sit in and protect in the middle. That's where the wing-backs can come in and help you. But the wing-backs have got to be unbelievably fit too, because they're doing a lot of work going back and forward. Often if you've got one of your two wider centre-halves going wide it can cause a bit of a problem and leave holes in the middle. A good example is when Aston Villa beat Manchester City 1–0 in December 2023. The scoreline doesn't tell the story because Villa were brilliant and could have won by more. City's Joško Gvardiol was playing on the left of a three and Leon Bailey, who scored the winner, was causing him all sorts of problems. The best players can learn from these things and improve, though. Gvardiol played a similar role in later games and got much better at it.

Tactically there's no question that you can learn from experience. An example is when Pep Guardiola was managing

Bayern Munich and they went to Barcelona in the Champions League semi-final in 2015 – the Nou Camp was a place he knew very well, of course. Bayern's back three of Jérôme Boateng, Mehdi Benatia and Rafinha were given the task of man-marking Neymar, Luis Suárez and Messi. They got destroyed 3–0. There are not many times Pep Guardiola has been destroyed. Bayern won the home leg 3–2 but it wasn't enough.

If you play four at the back, with two centre-backs rather than three, teams are less likely to throw three men up against two because they will be short somewhere behind. You have to adapt to the players you have, though. I was never wedded to three or four at the back as a principle in itself, and at Aston Villa I played four just because that suited the players we had, and it worked well for us.

Another way defensive tactics have changed is that lots of teams now have more and more specialist coaches, like the set-piece coach, which was unheard of until recently. Jürgen Klopp at Liverpool even had a throw-in coach! I tend to think all of that should still be part of the manager's job, and that of his general coaching staff. Creating too many roles can mean there is no accountability, and players might be given too many instructions and don't remember the basics. When it came to set-pieces we would have some sessions in pre-season, but not a dedicated coach, although my coaches would help come up with ideas. Steve Walford was a really good coach and helped organise my teams for set-pieces.

I had players that could come and head the ball, but things

were fairly simple. For defensive set-pieces, I used to say to my best header of the ball, 'You're free, and you're not marking anybody. You are going to go and take the flight of the ball and try to head it away. If you miss the header that's too bad, but you're going to try.' Generally speaking, that was Steve Walsh or Matt Elliott at Leicester, and Bobo Baldé at Celtic. It worked pretty well. With Brian Clough we never practised free-kicks or corners. He just wanted the best players to head the ball, either into the net from our corner, or away from our goal on theirs. Clough always used to tell us off if he thought we were 'on the outside looking in', in other words were being too passive. He wasn't very demonstrative when we won, which is not to say that he wasn't extremely happy about winning the game – he just showed it in his own way. He'd get you to settle down, and then point to someone and say, 'You won that for us today.' You felt great if he meant you.

Defensive tactics have certainly evolved a lot, and there have been some positive changes. The game is much less violent overall than in my day, and defenders have to use their skill and pace rather than just rely on hacking players down. This can sometimes go too far the other way, of course, and you lose that physicality which is part of the game. But there were some horrible tackles in my day that ruined careers. Now it is a faster game. I am interested to see how defensive tactics change as we move into the future, because football is always evolving. There has been an obsession in recent times with passing out from the back, putting defenders and goalkeepers into trouble. It sometimes seems like teams want to take more risks in their own penalty area than the opposition's. I hope this will be replaced with defenders defending, then getting it forward to their teammates in attack. That is what the supporters want to see, and what I want to see too.

6

ATTACKING

The other side of tactics is attack: breaking down opponents, getting the ball forward, putting it in the back of the net. There have been some major changes over my time in the game, and some people think football used to be just about getting the ball forward, but that's not quite right, there was always more nuance than that. It is fair to say, though, that football was generally more direct in the 1970s and 1980s, and that it has got progressively less so over time – but I'm not sure that is always a good thing. Attacking football now can be very indirect, which isn't the best to watch, and I don't think is always the best way of winning football matches.

The core of attacking play when I was a footballer was the wingers. Wingers would generally play on their stronger side, so for me, as a right-footed wide midfielder or winger, I would play on the right. Most good teams had wingers who could take people on and try to cross it in. That was the foundation of many attacks – getting the ball out wide, then getting it back in again quickly. At Nottingham Forest I was more of a wide midfield player than a winger because I liked to cut inside and tuck into the pitch, which gave us a slightly lopsided tactical approach. John Robertson was the focal point of the team as the left-winger and we would try to get the ball to him as often as we could. Then we had players in the middle like Archie Gemmill, Ian Bowyer and John McGovern. Being over on the right-hand side was often difficult: it was less crowded, so I was having to make runs all the time. Viv Anderson was an attacking right-back and when he got the ball he would just charge up the field. I would be supporting him, but if he lost the ball while I was up the pitch alongside him my job would be to get back again. There was a lot of running up and down. Overlapping full-backs, as you'd call them now, were coming into vogue at the time, with players like Viv and Terry Cooper at Leeds being the quintessential examples. They could offer a lot going forward but it was hard work being the midfield player in front of them because you were constantly having to track back. You had to be very fit to be a winger in those days, as you still do, of course.

As a winger if you did beat your man and get the ball into the box, you might have two people to aim at because teams often played with two strikers, which is relatively uncommon now. The old-fashioned strike partnership would be a big lad and a small lad, which you very rarely see in the modern game. Teams prefer to have an additional body in midfield, or wide forwards, rather than two out-and-out centre-forwards. In 1971 Kevin Keegan was just coming to the fore after joining Liverpool from Scunthorpe and formed a partnership with John Toshack. The pair were a classic little-and-large combination, with Toshack being the big strong Welshman, and Keegan small and agile all around him. It was a successful double act and that Liverpool team vied with Leeds to be the best side in the country at the time.

Player Roles

Brian Clough was big on people having set roles and sticking to them. He would never have heard of Bill Belichick, now one of the most celebrated head coaches in the history of American football after winning six Super Bowls with the New England Patriots, but they had something in common. The gist of Belichick's big thing when talking to players was: 'First of all know your job, and if you don't know what your job is, come and ask me and I will tell you, and then you do it.' Brian Clough preached exactly the same thing when he was my manager at Nottingham Forest: 'Do your job.' If that is to get the ball and give it to another player, that's fine, that's your job. He was big on players sticking to their set roles and not getting pulled out of position or doing things beyond the set roles. He would tell Viv Anderson that getting forward is lovely – if you've got the athleticism, that's fantastic – but your first job is to defend. If you want to be a central midfield player, you've got to have energy and be able to support your teammates, particularly in the centre of the pitch.

ATTACKING

For wide midfield players like me, our job was to get up and down the pitch. I had to keep doing that: it was the job I had been asked to do, and it required strong lungs. When John Robertson had the ball on the left-hand side, I was instructed to get to the back post and try to get the ball in the back of the net. I scored a decent number of goals in my career, including 48 in 285 games for Forest. Lots of them came about in exactly the same way, popping up at the back post from a John Robertson cross. My other big job, of course, was to get back immediately if a move broke down. It meant I would have to cover immense distances, perhaps more than anybody else on the pitch. I had to be very fit. These tactics worked well for us because John was the fulcrum of the team as our playmaker. He was essentially right-footed but he played left-wing. Lots of our other players – Archie Gemmill, Garry Birtles, Tony Woodcock, Ian Bowyer – were left-footed, but I was not. What happened was that when they played little triangles, all of those players naturally turned towards the left, so everything was going down that side. I was stranded out on the right having to make runs and wondering who was going to play it in, but often nobody did. When I did get the ball I would usually be looking to try to get it to a centre-forward, but often they were over on the left, so I was fairly isolated. That was the tactical approach we generally used in attack under Brian Clough at Nottingham Forest, which wasn't part of some overarching philosophy but was him using the tools he had, and adapting to the strengths and weaknesses of the players in the squad.

I tried to take that approach into my career in management. There is never a one-size-fits-all approach to winning a football match. Over time I optimised my tactics depending on the players I had and the team I was managing. I was always a big fan of adapting to circumstance: at Celtic in league games we would tend to have the majority of the ball and our tactics would be all about trying to break down teams that would sit deep. At Aston Villa we were in that position against some teams, perhaps the clubs that had just got promoted, but against the biggest teams the shoe would be on the other foot and we would be looking to sit back and hit them on the break.

I had to think hard about attacking tactics and how I wanted to win when I arrived at Villa Park, because although it was a big club with lots of history, I didn't think the squad I inherited was particularly strong. The season before I arrived they'd finished 16th, only just avoiding relegation, so my first season was about keeping our heads above water as much as anything else. Big improvements came after some great attacking signings: players like Stiliyan Petrov in midfield, from my former club Celtic, John Carew up front, and Ashley Young on the wing. It took a while or so for things to properly click and the next season we came 11th, which was progress. The following season we were really good, coming sixth in 2007–08, and finishing in the same position for the subsequent two seasons, qualifying for Europe three times in a row, which was great for the club.

A lot of why that Villa side got better over time was simply because we had better players going forward like the ones I've mentioned. Our midfielders, including Gareth Barry and James Milner, made big contributions too. When it comes to tactics in an attacking sense, my view is that if you've got good players, they should eventually be able to win you a game. Of course, things can go wrong, and luck can go against you. But more than often it holds true: if you have good attacking players and they play to the best of their ability, they will win the game for you.

Although the best players usually win you matches, there are some things you can do to make that more likely. For example, I wanted at least some players in my team with the ability to take defenders on one-on-one. I think that is really important. The reason I bought Ashley Young at Aston Villa is because I knew he could take players on; he could run at people and dribble past them. James Milner started out as a wide player but I brought him into central midfield because I thought that was where his strengths lay. He wasn't so much a player for one-on-ones but was a strong running player, brave and could go up and down all day long. Those qualities meant he was wasted on the wide right-hand side, especially as we had players like Young and Gabriel Agbonlahor who were brilliant at running with the ball and beating players out by the touchline. We were solid in midfield and had a lot of pace, so I felt we always had a chance in games, even against very good teams. If you could just sit in, keep things tight and then hit teams with pace on the break, there was always a chance of getting a result. I remember a 2–0 away win at Arsenal where we just kept hitting them again and again with the pace of Young and Agbonlahor. Counter-attacking football is sometimes seen as a negative thing but it can be really exciting when you do it right – defending smartly, absorbing pressure, and then stunning the opposition with power and pace in attack. That win in November 2008 started a great run and we were in the top three after Christmas, but couldn't quite maintain the lead – maybe we didn't have a big enough squad for it. That Villa team was built on pace and quick attacks and we felt we could beat anyone on the right day.

It isn't always as neat as saying that the best teams hog possession and smaller teams counter-attack. Manchester United under Sir Alex Ferguson were a counter-attacking side a lot of the time. They could sit back, absorb pressure, and then hit you with their attacking players. They were able to turn that defence into attack quite quickly, it wasn't necessarily about dominating possession. Usually, though, the best teams want to keep the ball, which is nothing new. The great Liverpool teams of the 1970s and 1980s were masters at keeping possession, although the state of pitches back then meant the whole approach had to be slightly different. The back-pass rule certainly helped. Arsène Wenger's Arsenal sides were very good at keeping the ball too. But this tactical approach was supercharged by the arrival in England of Pep Guardiola, who brought the blueprint of hugely successful Spain and Barcelona teams to Manchester City, helped by the fact that by the time he arrived English pitches were near enough perfect in the depths of winter and you could knock the ball along the grass all day long. For a while I think the pendulum swung too far in one direction because

City were so dominant and the obsession with keeping the ball came to be seen as the 'right' way to play football, which just won't work with all players. You would sometimes see lesser teams getting the ball high up the pitch and passing it sideways, not attacking the space, and being slow and ponderous with no bite at all, and maybe getting the ball taken off them. When you have a team packed with players like Kevin De Bruyne and Erling Haaland you will generally find a way through and score. But other teams try it and just don't go anywhere; they get closed down and play it right back to the goalkeeper. It can be so frustrating to watch. Southampton came to the Premier League in 2024–25 and tried to play that kind of football and almost broke Derby County's record for the lowest points total in Premier League history. Fans do not want to see their team get 60 or 70 per cent possession and lose. They want to win games, even if they have less of the ball. I've heard some TV pundits talking about the Manchester City team being less strong with Haaland in it. I don't share that opinion. He has scored so many goals for them. That is what matters, not complicated passing that doesn't result in goals.

When I think back to things that I would insist my team carried out in attack, another was players getting to the near post. It irritates me when I watch games now and don't see this happening. If play suddenly breaks down, and a player wins the ball high up the pitch and manages to get a cross in, I want to see someone attacking the near post. That can either be the centre-forward or a midfield player, it doesn't matter who, just someone needs to get there. I find it frustrating when players wait in the middle of the penalty box for a tap-in, because it's much harder to make that cross than one to the near post. The further a player is from the near post, the more difficult it is for the player crossing the ball to reach him, especially if he is being closed down. I think back to that time Brian Clough yelled at me for playing my teammate into trouble with a bad one-two. Make it easy for your teammate. The other advantage of hitting the near post is that if nobody connects with it, the ball will come zipping across the goal and hopefully one of your other players can connect with it, or you could force an own goal – you're keeping the ball alive. If you aim long and miss, the move is over. That is why I always emphasised that if there was a cross my players should attack the near post and be expecting the cross there.

In my playing days John Robertson was one of the great crossers in the game with his left foot. He would just whip it in. He would tell us that he was not pinpointing those passes: he had too much on his plate and didn't have time to look up and see who was in the penalty box and where. He was trying to get a ball with a bit of whip, bending away from the goalkeeper and into the dangerous area at the near post. Kevin De Bruyne at his best was excellent at this. When he got the ball he would whip it in, and whether it was Erling Haaland or another player, it would be up to them to make the move and attack the near post. This is a simple idea but it is as relevant today as it has ever been.

ATTACKING

When I think about the brilliant attacking football I have been a part of, both as a player and as a manager, I think about some of the best moments and best players. The best player I've played with is John Robertson, undoubtedly. He changed position from being a central midfield player to playing out wide, which demands courage to deal with the ball in tight situations. He always said that the great thing about playing wide was that the touchline was his friend, because there was nobody on the other side who was going to take the ball off him. John loved the touchline. He said he could see the whole game from that position. As a winger on the other side, I wanted to play inside more. I wasn't slow, but you need that explosive burst of pace to get past players and whip it in, which I didn't have in the way John did. I could do it occasionally, and liked to surprise a full-back who might think I was coming inside, but then I would go outside. Usually my preference was cutting inside, though, which was the source of lots of my goals, including that special one against Manchester United at Old Trafford in 1971. Archie Gemmill was another fantastic attacking midfielder I played with, who will always be remembered for his goal for Scotland against the Netherlands in 1978, one of the best ever scored at the World Cup.

The best attacking player I managed was probably Henrik Larsson, because he scored so many goals but was also a great team player. Some centre-forwards are selfish, but he would happily square the ball if someone else was in a better position. I always think of him as a really brave player too, ready to stick his head in if it might lead to a goal. He was a really fine player, and his goalscoring record was extraordinary: 174 goals in 221 Celtic games, most of them during my time. In my first full season he scored 53 goals in 50 games as we won the domestic treble, which is an incredible memory. You can talk all you like about the different attributes and strengths players possess, but a player who is scoring more than one goal every game is worth their weight in gold. Another attacking player I remember particularly fondly is Steve Guppy because I was with him for such a long time and we went on a journey together. I managed him at Wycombe where we got promoted twice, then signed him at Leicester where we won the League Cup, and then again at Celtic where we won the league. He was a really good player with a lovely left foot and could whip the ball in very accurately. In the 1998–99 season he was the only player in the whole division to play every minute, something outfield players don't manage very often. As a manager you love a player who is always available.

Freedom Versus Control

I always wanted my best attackers to play with an element of freedom and not be second-guessing themselves every time they had the ball in the opponent's half. Players can feel under pressure to plan how they're going to use the ball before they receive it, but it is important to retain a degree of spontaneity and surprise. Everyone thinks they know how their opponent plays, and there is so much footage and information available these days that a player can feel almost remote-controlled, with no individual agency. In the modern game players aren't trusted enough to make their own decisions. There is a risk of losing the very essence of football and stifling a player's best qualities. If you are over-coaching them, constantly telling them where to stand and what pass to make, you run the risk of them losing all the important skills of how to think on their feet. I was never a believer in micromanaging attacking moves or drilling into players *exactly* what they should do with the ball if they get it in a certain area of the pitch. Of course, no matter how much of a maverick you are, you need some sort of discipline when you've lost the ball and need to get back. But with those maverick players I always wanted to encourage them to get on the ball and make something happen. I think back to some of the mavericks from my playing career. George Best, of course, but also Stan Bowles, who Queens Park Rangers fans still talk about, as well as Frank Worthington, Bobby Charlton and Denis Law.

I am a believer in transmitting just the most important things so as not to overwhelm a player with information. That is a Brian Clough idea that I believe still holds true today – at every level of football, not just in the Premier League. From a very young age children are overwhelmed with information in every aspect of life, including football. They are being told what to do with the ball before they receive it rather than figuring it out for themselves. There are fewer dribblers because they can't develop that skill if they are always told to pass the ball. Imagine if Messi, when he was eight years old, had been constantly told by his coaches to pass the ball rather than run with it. We wouldn't have had Messi. At that sort of age football should be more about enjoying yourself. If you tell a seven- or eight-year-old to make a diagonal run, or cover defensively, he will probably get it wrong and not enjoy it. He's seven years old. Let him play with the ball, make some mistakes, and when he is 14 or 15 we can start correcting things.

In terms of practising attacking football – and I suppose defensive football as well – I was a big believer in small-sided games rather than always playing on a full-size pitch. Lots of players I coached enjoyed those too. Steve Guppy still uses them at the teams in America he's been coaching. I liked little drills like that, which I thought were brilliant for multiple things: fitness, skills, getting players to understand each other. My favourite one involves a 25-yard square area marked with balls or cones and a goal at either end. It is simple: one-versus-one plus a goalkeeper at each end. The player tries to score. If he loses the ball he has to run back very quickly. If the goalkeeper saves it the player will be wanting him to give it out quickly. It is lightning fast, it only lasts about two minutes, but a player's legs have completely gone in that time. That game was absolutely great for dribblers of the ball, people like Ashley Young, who loved it. It's not for everyone – some players hated it; it is hard work. You can change things up when players are getting tired by going two-on-two rather than one-on-one, but you wouldn't want anything bigger than that. That game had absolutely everything in it and was great fun. Barcelona did similar things in Messi's time, playing short games rather than always working on a big pitch.

Of course, you can't do that all the time and there is a stage where you have to do some proper fitness work, especially in pre-season. But games like that are helpful because they make you practise getting the ball back. Guardiola's big idea of dominating possession is partly based on the reasoning: if you have the ball in a game, your workload is cut down a lot. That might sound like stating the obvious, but it is an important insight – it is much more tiring when you are trying to retrieve the ball than when your team is passing it around. Part of the secret of Guardiola's success when he was manager of Barcelona was getting that ball back within ten or 15 seconds. Once a team has the ball back, you have players who can deal with it, who can create opportunities, but also look after the ball, slow things down and let your players have a rest while your opponents are sprinting around trying to take it off you. The important thing is possession with purpose, not just hogging the ball for the sake of it – and that Barcelona side certainly always had purpose. When Xavi, Iniesta and Messi were playing, I tried to watch Barcelona as often as I could because the creativity in the side was terrific. You knew they could always make something happen. They moved the ball in a way in which even a back pass seemed a forward-thinking move. They occasionally went backwards, but only to keep possession and go forward. They weren't counting the passes they made, or trying to run up possession statistics – there was always a purpose to their play, and it was just brilliant. Messi would sometimes give and receive the ball two or three times, just short passes, and you knew that in his mind he would be thinking about something a bit further ahead. At some point he would pass it and move and find himself in a brilliant position.

Guardiola's teams at Manchester City were wonderful to watch as well. Again, there was always a purpose to them passing the ball, at least when they were at their very best. Kevin De Bruyne's passing was incredible; he is one of the best midfield players there has ever been in the Premier League, so direct and always keen to get the ball into dangerous areas. I loved watching De Bruyne on the half-turn, always moving towards the opposition goal and looking to make a dangerous pass, never content to just pass it sideways or backwards.

In a different sort of way I also really enjoyed watching Jürgen Klopp's teams. They were different in style: gung-ho, get-up-and-at-them, and powered on by the crowd as much as anything else. Klopp had eight full seasons at Liverpool and only lost four home Premier League games in that time with an Anfield crowd – excluding a run of six consecutive defeats during the pandemic, when they went through a terrible period with no fans in the stadium. It shows you the importance of the stadium and a noisy home crowd, which can influence the type of football you play. It's a bit like at Celtic: you can have a plan, but you know that whatever it is, the crowd will ultimately dictate things because they will want you to get forward and avoid passing it around at the back. Often at Celtic we just drove forward in the matches, spurred on by the crowd, which is how we did so well domestically while also getting some brilliant results in Europe.

You would have a plan before the game but, as a manager, I would not be imparting detailed information to the players in my team talk. At the same time, though, I thought it was important that the last voice the players would hear before running out was a voice hopefully of some substance, and I would be able to influence them a little bit. They would only be able to remember the vague impression and tone of what I would say, not intricate tactical details: after ten or 15 minutes, whatever you've said to them will have rubbed off, you're just hoping they will be focused from minute one of the game.

Best Opponents

Thinking about how attacking football has changed over the decades, one of the most exciting sides to watch was the Brazil side that won the 1970 World Cup. They were perhaps the best international side of all time, and I was fortunate enough to play against them. In 1973 they were on tour in Europe, with a side still including about six of the team that had won the World Cup. They were preparing for the World Cup the following year in Germany. I wasn't playing for Northern Ireland but rather for an all-Ireland team – Ireland plus Northern Ireland – which was a big deal at the time because the politics were fractious. I was very young but was lucky enough to get picked. We had to be called a 'Shamrock Rovers XI' rather than 'All-Ireland' because Northern Ireland's football association had objected to that. Whatever our name was, it was a fantastic opportunity to play against those Brazilians in Dublin. Pelé had just retired, unfortunately, but I got the chance to play against lots of the greats including Jairzinho, who scored in every round at the 1970 World Cup, making him the only player ever to do so all the way to the final. They also had a boy called Rivellino, with a big moustache and a brilliant left foot, who was a key part of the 1970 team. Another one was Clodoaldo, who played a big role in maybe the most famous World Cup goal of all time. He dribbled past four players before the ball went up the field and Carlos Alberto finished a wonderful team sequence when they demolished Italy 4–1 in the final. I still have his shirt from that game against Brazil. We lost 4–3 in the end but were pretty happy to score three goals, the first team to have done so against Brazil for eight years. They were just too strong in attack. But the preparation didn't do them much good. After winning three World Cups out of four with Pelé between 1958 and 1970 – the exception being England's victory in 1966 – Brazil failed to reach the final in 1974 after losing in the second round to another excellent side, a Johan Cruyff-inspired Netherlands.

That Dutch side of the 1970s were incredible tactically, introducing 'Total Football' to the world, the idea that every player could play in every position. Total Football had a big impact on the game going forward because players at the top level all over the world became much more fluid and versatile and moved around the pitch more. It was perhaps the precursor to the modern game where defenders play more of a role in attack, attackers defend by pressing from the front, and even goalkeepers get involved in attack by playing a role in build-up play. The world of attacking tactics owes a great deal to that Dutch side. They reached the World Cup final in 1974 and 1978 but lost both, to West Germany followed by Argentina, making the Dutch side one of the best teams never to win the tournament.

In between those two World Cups we played against the Netherlands twice. In the first game in October 1976 we drew 2–2 in Rotterdam, which was a great result, although I didn't play. Cruyff scored one of their goals. I did play in the return fixture where, unfortunately, we lost 1–0. They had some brilliant players: not just Cruyff but also Johnny Rep, Johan Neeskens, and the captain Ruud Krol, coached, of course, by Rinus Michels, who made such an impact on Tony Woodcock. The player that really sticks in my memory was Wim van Hanegem, a very good midfield player who was part of the Feyenoord side that won the European Cup in 1970. Those Dutch players were smart and skilful but could be quite aggressive. They could look after themselves and dish it out physically.

Unfortunately, Cruyff didn't play in the 1978 World Cup following a kidnap attempt on his family, something that was only revealed decades later. I was lucky enough to work with Cruyff as a pundit a couple of times before he sadly died in 2016. Not only did he know everything about the game, but if you had an opinion on it, he was prepared to listen. He wasn't one of those to argue just for the sake of it, or put you down. He was very impressive in that respect, considering what a player and manager he was. He was widely influential on Pep Guardiola and other managers who've liked their players to be positionally fluid.

Another great attacking side I played against was France in the 1982 World Cup. They had Michel Platini, one of the all-time greats, but also some other top players like Patrick Battiston and Dominique Rocheteau. I fondly remember Alain Giresse, who was a fabulous footballer and scored two against us in that 4–1 defeat in Spain 1982, as did Rocheteau.

Thinking back to my time as a manager, one of the best attacking players I came up against was Thierry Henry. He started out as a wide player because he was so quick but, over time, Arsène Wenger converted him into more of a striker. I was in the dugout at Highbury for his debut against Leicester on the opening day of the 1999–2000 season. He came on as a half-time sub and must have been clean through about six times. He kept missing the chances but you knew he was going to be brilliant – you wouldn't necessarily have guessed he would go on to score all the goals that he did, but you knew he was going to get in behind people and be a special player.

Defence Into Attack

Defenders today are much more involved in the attacking build-up in two main ways: in passing the ball out and in carrying the ball out. These days teams really like to have one left-footed and one right-footed centre-back, which gives you a nice balance and makes it easier for them to make long passes forward with their preferred foot. If you have two right-footed centre-backs they are always turning and passing in the same direction. A left-footer gives you some variety. Passing centre-backs are nothing new, though. The Liverpool side I came up against lots of times, which dominated European football for a while, had defenders like Mark Lawrenson and Alan Hansen, or even Graeme Souness as a defensive midfielder, who could all absolutely pass the ball as well as run with it out from the back. One of the players I managed, Matty Elliott, sticks in the memory as being incredibly good with the ball at his feet. Many would see him as a big lump of a centre-half but he was much more than that. It has often been the centre-back that comes out with the ball; that isn't a tactical innovation either. Hansen and Lawrenson were known at Liverpool for running out of defence with the ball as well as passing it forward. The master of it was Franz Beckenbauer, of course, the great German defender famous for his forward runs.

Another big shift in attacking tactics that might surprise younger readers is how defenders frequently go forward for attacking set-pieces. That seems an obvious thing to do now, but it rarely happened when I started out. The first big centre-half I remember going up for corner kicks was Jack Charlton at Leeds United. He used to stand right by the keeper and try to prod him into the net. With the ball coming in, if Charlton could nudge the keeper before he got to it, it would often lead to a goal. Lots of those goals would probably be disallowed these days. I remember another lad called Charlie Hurley at Sunderland way back in the 1960s who would come up for corners because he was good in the air. It was quite innovative at the time because a defender's job at corners was to stay back. But now, of course, lots of defenders will come up for corners because heading the ball in defence and in attack requires pretty much the same skill. These days, even with VAR and all the TV cameras, corners can still be very physical. Arsenal under Mikel Arteta have made set-pieces a speciality and you see their players blocking goalkeepers, presumably coming quite close to committing fouls each time but usually getting away with it, even when it looks like they're grappling with their opponent. Goalkeepers have always been under pressure at corner kicks. Early in my playing career, Jim Barron was our goalkeeper at Forest and he was quite a handsome chap and didn't like to get his face hurt, which I don't think helped.

ATTACKING

Just as we would think a lot about how best to deal with set-pieces defensively, we would view them as an opportunity going forward as well. With Celtic we had a lot of dangerous players to get on the end of a dead-ball situation, like Henrik Larsson, Chris Sutton, John Hartson and our big centre-half Bobo Baldé, who was our best header of the ball. The opposition tended to send their best marker to him and he would be taken out of the game. We would tell him to just stand there and not attack the ball, but Larsson was brilliant in the air and so was Chris Sutton, so we had players coming across at different angles. We scored a lot of goals that way, but the planning behind it was never too complicated. Things are far more intricate now, with set-piece coaches and whatever else.

Set-pieces aren't the most aesthetically pleasing way to score a goal, but they are very important, especially if you are the underdog struggling to break the team down in open play. In such games I would always tell my players that a set-piece was a golden opportunity and that we should make the most of them and take our time, because no team in the world likes defending set-pieces. Another thing I would tell my players was that you can psychologically gain something from a set-piece even if you don't score a goal. Say you win the ball with a big, towering header that goes just over the bar – your opponents will be concerned about the next one. You can get inside their heads. Funnily enough, as football becomes more about intricate passing and skilful touches, set-pieces can actually become more important and effective. Against that amazing Barcelona side, who were so skilful and technically adept, you always felt their Achilles heel was defending set-pieces because they weren't a physically imposing team. Size really matters when it comes to set-pieces, and having big lads at corners and free-kicks is a way you can get a small advantage over a team that might be technically better.

One of my best results as Celtic manager was a 1–1 draw with Barcelona at the Nou Camp in the Champions League in 2004, a few months after we had beaten them over two legs in the UEFA Cup. Our teenage goalkeeper David Marshall had been incredible in those games. In the later Champions League game they went a goal up through Samuel Eto'o but we equalised just before half-time. The goal came from a set-piece. Stiliyan Petrov swung in a wide free-kick, Stanislav Varga flicked it on and John Hartson poked it in at the back post. If you watch it back, it was a good ball but all their defenders just missed it, and Carles Puyol – a brilliant defender, of course, who won everything there is to win – made a hash of the clearance. When you are up against a top team it is much easier to ask those questions of defenders through set-pieces than from open play. The goal in that amazing win for Ireland against Germany in Dublin wasn't quite from a set-piece but it came about when our keeper sent the ball all the way downfield and Shane Long ran on to it, running past Mats Hummels and shooting past the keeper. Some of the game's star defenders still don't like a bouncing ball, and something like this can give an attacker their one opportunity in a game. Even against the very best players in the world you tend to get at least one opportunity.

When I think about the best attacking players nowadays, one thing I wonder about is how George Best would have fitted into it all. He might have scored as many goals – perhaps even more with better players around him, on better pitches, and with better protection from referees – but, at the same time, he might not have shone so brightly in today's game as he did in his own career, which briefly overlapped with my own in Northern Ireland. There seem to be fewer mavericks like George Best in today's game. Maybe it's because the tactics are a lot more rigid and that kind of flair gets coached out of players a bit. Best was famous for his escapades off the pitch, and that might have been the downfall of him. In the modern game if you're up to that sort of thing people are going to know about it a lot more quickly. But George Best was a special talent and I think he would have thrived in any team in any era. As I have said a few times now, the simple things never change: have the better players and get the ball to them and you will probably win. Not always, though, which is why our game is so exciting.

When it comes to attacking tactics the constants won't change. You want to have players that can take people on, attack the posts, and get it forward rather than just passing it around at the back all the time. Things will change in other ways, though, of course they will. The game won't stop evolving. Maybe in 40 years' time people will look back on today's matches and think the pace is impossibly slow. You don't have to go back into ancient history to recognise that: even if you watch Premier League games from the 2000s there is a lot more long-ball action and it all seems slower. The game is constantly shifting, and we can't predict all the developments that will happen, but the essence of the game hasn't changed as much as you might think.

7

TRANSFERS

For most of my career the business of signing players was pretty much the manager's job, and the manager's job only. The chairman had to sign off the money, of course, and at Nottingham Forest the assistant manager Peter Taylor was highly influential in terms of players brought in, but it was a small circle of people involved at any club. Things have changed massively in that respect. The top clubs employ so many people to carry out analysis and scouting now. Having more brains going into the operation can be good, but I worry the people making the decisions are not the ones carrying the can if things do not go well. In my days as a manager I never signed a player without seeing him with my own eyes. At some clubs nowadays it seems like the manager might not have any idea who is coming and who is going. Of course, a lot of players you may not need to scout extensively. If they play in your league you have seen them play and don't need to do lots of research to decide if they're going to be a good fit or not. But in other cases you do, particularly when signing players from abroad.

When I was at Aston Villa we spent quite a lot of money

on Ashley Young from Watford, who were also in the Premier League at the time. I went to see him play at Vicarage Road a couple of times, which was easy compared to seeing a player abroad. One game I watched, Watford saw very little of the ball, so it did not give the best indication of his strengths, but you could see that he had terrific natural ability. He turned out to be a great signing. Muzzy Izzet was another one of my best. I knew about him when I was Wycombe manager because I used to go and watch Chelsea reserves every other week at Kingstonian. He went on to become one of the core members of my Leicester team despite not being a high-profile player when I signed him. The crucial thing when signing players was that I had to go and see them play first. Somebody could be recommended to me, but eventually I would see him live before committing to signing him. That was really important to me.

These days perhaps the manager has too many things to do and can't always get to games, or perhaps he no longer has the ultimate say, and someone else in the club does instead. I always wanted the final say because the signing was going to affect me the most. If a new signing didn't work out, it would be me the owner would seek out about it, rather than any other member of staff. So I wanted to know as much as possible beforehand. Even now, with all the data available, teams are still making big mistakes on players. Some of the biggest clubs in the world have spent so much money in recent years on players who just do not look good enough to me. Manchester United are the obvious example. They have made some terrible decisions in the years since Sir Alex Ferguson left in 2013, the last time they won the league. The recruitment has not been good. They have spent huge sums and rarely improved.

People try to justify some signings by saying the players are young, so their value will supposedly go up, as if that's a reason in itself – but a young player who isn't good enough is going to be an older player who isn't good enough. I'm amazed at some of the signings made by top clubs these days – with all the wealth of data and analysis available – of players who just do not pass the eye test. Data is all well and good but you need to ask basic questions: can a player control the ball? Can a player run with the ball? I'm not sure data shows that definitively, and making a bad signing can have a long-term impact. Transfers are paid in instalments, so a big, wasted fee can tie your hands for years to come. I'm not sure some of the players that have moved for big sums of money in recent years have ever had the fundamentals you need as a top player, no matter what the data might say.

When it feels like a transfer isn't working out, it can be hard to know whether to keep persisting with the player, or just cut your losses. If you have a genuine belief that the player can improve you need to communicate that – the psychological aspect is very important. Stiliyan Petrov from Celtic was my first signing at Aston Villa. He had a wonderful debut against West Ham. He was simply marvellous. But then he lost his form, and it looked like it was going to be a real struggle for him. I got to a stage where I had a conversation with him and said I didn't think it was really going to work out at Villa. He asked me to give him another chance, so I did. And it wasn't an immediate improvement, but he gradually got better and better. He found his niche and style again, and ended up being terrific, a real stalwart of the Villa team, who was very popular with the fans. Sometimes it goes the other way, though. Nicky Shorey is another player I got in at Villa, a left-back from Reading, who we bought after Freddy Bouma broke his leg. He was a nice player and got in the England squad at one point, but it wasn't really working for him, so he moved on to West Bromwich Albion.

Discovering Talent

The process of scouting a player has changed massively over the last decade or two, and there is much more reliance on data and computer analysis now, which can have upsides, for sure. Teams like Brentford and Brighton have done really well with a data-driven approach. They've recruited admirably and got in fantastic managers, which has played a huge part in their success. What is particularly impressive about Brighton is they have weathered selling some of their best players, and continued to be excellent, moving on and unearthing the next hidden gem.

When it comes to using data in football, something I am always concerned about is the excessive focus on clips. When I was a manager looking at signing a player I would always ask my analysts to show me a recording of a whole game, and then it would be my job to watch it. I needed to see 90 minutes, not five clips from his agent of his best moments that skipped over all the stuff that is not so impressive. Then I'd head off to see the player in person, doing a fair bit of scouting abroad when the calendar allowed it. For example, at Celtic I signed Bobo Baldé, our big centre-back from Toulouse, having travelled over there twice before agreeing to sign him. I got lucky because they had midweek games in France when we happened to be free. I could see he was a big lad, exactly what I wanted: a defender who could defend and was strong in the air. Toulouse wanted £2.5 million for him at first, but we ended up getting him for free because they were in financial trouble: they were relegated and had to release him. He did really well for us.

Brian Clough relied a lot on his assistant Peter Taylor to pick players, and Taylor relied on Clough to manage them. They were a good combination in that respect. I think there were one or two players they signed without extensive scouting – like Trevor Francis from Birmingham City, who became the first ever million-pound player. That was never a risk because everyone knew Francis was top quality. With others they would do more research, going to watch them to see if they would fit into the team. Overall, these things have changed, and managers have less power in general and more staff are now involved in a transfer. With some exceptions, like Guardiola and Klopp in recent years, who have had huge power, managers generally have far less control than the likes of Brian Clough had. Lots of them are called 'head coaches' rather than managers now. I remember David Pleat, one of the early people to take on one of these advisory roles, including at Nottingham Forest, telling me it could be good for me because this person could act as the conduit between me and the board. I asked, 'What would prevent me from having a conversation with the board or the owner?' I did not need a conduit.

When I think back on transfer business in the various jobs I have had, at Wycombe I relied on my own eyes a lot and went to watch *a lot* of football matches. First of all I had to try to understand the strength of the Vauxhall Conference at the time. It was interesting to get up to speed with this because I had managed a couple of leagues below that at Grantham Town, and the difference in quality of players was significant, despite the gap only being a couple of divisions and still being in the world of non-league football where players had a day job. But there were some very good footballers at that level, and that is still the case today. As well as scouting teams in your division for possible signings, you are also watching them to figure out the best way to beat them.

Obviously the best way to find out about other teams is to play against them. I was lucky to arrive at Wycombe at a time when results in my first few months were not so important. This was a time when only one team went up from the Conference, and when I arrived in February 1990 we were way behind the leaders but comfortably clear of any relegation danger, so those first few fixtures were mostly about getting to know the players and the strength of the league. I realised the competition was really quite strong, more so than you might have expected if you'd spent your whole career in the top divisions. The best team in the league was Barnet, under Barry Fry, but there were lots of other good sides too. At Wycombe, when it came to signing players, I would just go and see the chairman, Ivor Beeks, and ask if we could afford to get someone in. We did pay money for players but the fees weren't high. There was a lot of haggling over prices because it affected the rest of our budget. The agreement with the other club would be something I would present to the chairman, and the final decision was up to him.

Of course, when I moved up the divisions there was more money involved, but still much less than there is today. When I joined Leicester City the chairman, Martin George, allowed me to sign centre-back Julian Watts from Sheffield Wednesday for £200,000. Muzzy Izzet joined from Chelsea, initially on loan. We hadn't been promoted at this point so didn't have a huge budget. When we went up to the Premier League we needed to strengthen the side and made a few signings in the summer but didn't spend much compared to modern teams. We bought goalkeeper Kasey Keller for £900,000 from Millwall, forward Ian Marshall for £800,000 from Ipswich Town, and centre-back Spencer Prior from Norwich for £600,000. This is small money, relatively speaking, considering today promoted teams might spend £100 million just to give themselves a chance, and even that may well not be enough. The transfer window didn't close in September back then so we could sign a few more players later in the season, including Matt Elliott from Oxford United for £1.6 million, which was one of the best signings I ever made, alongside Steve Guppy, the following month, a player I had managed at Wycombe who was at Port Vale at the time. We got him for £850,000, which proved a bargain for someone who went on to play so many games in the Premier League. Despite that relatively modest business in the 1996–97 season we finished ninth and won the League Cup. It's hard to imagine a promoted team doing the same now with similar levels of spending. The difference in quality between promoted sides and established Premier League sides seems increasingly vast, and it is so hard for promoted teams to stay up unless they spend vast sums of money, which is difficult with the new profit and sustainability rules (PSR) that have been brought in.

Over time I brought in a lot of good players at Leicester. Alongside the players named above I signed Steve Claridge, Gerry Taggart and Theo Zagorakis – all good signings, so people hopefully thought I knew what I was doing. You are never going to get everything right, but I did look after the money at Leicester, and hopefully at all the clubs I managed. I always tried to treat the money as if it was my own. Even with Celtic, a big club with a huge stadium and global fanbase, affordability was the main concern when it came to signings. The manager chose the players – nobody really questioned me there in that sense – but, again, we did not have a huge budget.

As well as trying to watch players myself, I relied on my scouts, who are employed by the club to go and watch players rather than just analyse them on a laptop. They send in reports and then hopefully the manager will go and see the player. You would be relying on a scout being able to watch the player a number of times, so a geographical spread was important. At Nottingham Forest we had a scout in the north-east of England, the north-west and down south.

Now there are fewer scouts, as I would think of them, and more analysts, people with skills in data and analytics, sometimes without football backgrounds. You would still hope that the manager would go and watch a player if there was a chance to sign him, but I think a lot of that has disappeared now because lots of analysts are on computer systems where you can analyse games all over the world. Maybe that's good because you can watch a game in South America, for example, which might be very difficult to do otherwise. If you watch two or three of those games, you should be in a position to tell the manager that, if he can make the time, he should go and have a look – although that's highly unlikely at that distance. These days at the top teams, almost all the players they sign from abroad are already very well known. Nobody disputed Manchester City spending a big fee on Erling Haaland because his record in Germany for Borussia Dortmund was clear. He didn't need a great deal of scouting. All they had to do was find the money. I know analysts now use much more data in terms of statistics. Not just goals, but assists, expected goals, all of that. That has changed a lot. It was more your eye and your instinct that you relied on in my day. Managers today have a lot more help, but I think they should spend time watching football matches on tape after training, particularly those involving potential recruits;

that should reap dividends. The manager gets praised or blamed for transfer business, so he should have the main responsibility for the decisions.

When I went to Celtic in 2000, the chairman Dermot Desmond said he wanted me to be in control of the club, which was great. I don't mean financially, just in terms of running the football side of things. He said he held great store in his businesses and his managers, which was why he employed them to do the job. That was music to my ears. I spoke to him often, but he let me get on with things in general. He wouldn't come to the training ground, or many league games, but he would come to the big ones like the Old Firm matches and our European games. He was running other businesses at the same time so wouldn't have time to get involved in everything, which is what you want as a manager. I owed him a great deal, because there were other big names in for the job at the time. I was doing well at Leicester but was a relative unknown compared to others. He took a chance on me and I am very grateful for that. I was very happy at Leicester and wouldn't have moved for a lot of clubs, but Celtic was one of them, considering my background in Northern Ireland.

There were other big clubs I had the chance to manage at various times. West Ham was one, Leeds was another, but they didn't happen for various reasons, although I'm not sitting around regretting things. At Celtic I always felt in control of the transfer business, but I started to notice big changes by the time I was at Sunderland between 2011 and 2013, where I was not in control. I might recommend a player, but there were lots of other people involved. It was the first time I had felt opposition to potential transfer targets, although that was perhaps true in my latter stages at Aston Villa too. Sunderland was a real eye-opener behind the scenes though. I did not rate the owner or the chief executive; I do not mind saying that.

Nowadays the increase of data allows teams to do so much tracking of players – the distance they've covered, their heart rate, that sort of thing. But you have to be careful if you're going to judge a player on things like that. Some players charge around the pitch and never get a kick. Also, if someone has covered a bit more ground than someone else, it might mean their positioning is bad. Some of the best centre-backs don't need to move around that much because they always know exactly where the ball is. These statistics depend a lot on position too: if you're a coach you should be able to tell that someone playing wide as a wing-back is going to cover a lot more ground than a centre-half. He's going to go backwards and forwards. So the data can be good, but you need to know how to use it – and have an eye for the game and a feeling for it that comes with experience.

Although I have been a bit critical of the world of data and analysis, I did rely on some excellent people in that respect in my time in management. Paddy Riley was my analysis man at Aston Villa, and he did really well for me – although more in terms of preparing for games and figuring out what to do during games, rather than when it came to signing players. I'd ask him about something that happened in the first half and he would get it up on a screen as quickly as possible so we could have a look at it with the players. That was between 2006 and 2010 so, of course, it's all much more sophisticated now, but I think there is always a risk of information overload that comes with that approach. You've got almost unlimited data, but there are only 15 minutes at half-time when everything is so frantic. Players can only take in so much; if you overload them they will remember nothing.

Rivals

One funny story about a transfer comes to mind. I was trying to sign Dwight Yorke at Celtic. It was a couple of years after he had left Manchester United and he was at Blackburn at the time. He was coming up to Glasgow very late on deadline day to do his medical. There were no obvious issues and we thought he was about to sign on loan until the end of the season. But he had been in touch with Steve Bruce, who was then the manager of Birmingham City. Bruce had convinced Yorke to go there instead of Celtic. They needed Yorke's signature and wanted to use Celtic's fax machine to do the deal! Steve Bruce himself asked me if he could use it. Unbelievable. I can laugh about it now, but I didn't find it funny at the time!

It's quite normal to get annoyed with other clubs and other managers about transfers, because you're competing directly against each other. I've mentioned how it felt like Liverpool were trying to destabilise Gareth Barry over a period of time at Villa Park. That sort of thing is always going to happen. I think you just have to treat it as part of the game. Sometimes you will be on the other side of it too, doing something in the transfer market that annoys other teams. It's best not to moan about these things but just get on with it.

Transfers can quite often be as much about weakening rivals as strengthening your own team. When Newcastle's Saudi takeover happened and they brought in Eddie Howe, the club was in real danger of relegation. They bought New Zealand native Chris Wood, a reliable striker from Burnley. This was not just because it would help Newcastle but because it would harm their relegation rivals. It worked: Burnley's main goal source dried up and they went down. A similar thing happened to Aston Villa during my time there, and afterwards. Garry Cook at Manchester City later admitted they had a plan to weaken Villa, who they needed to overtake in those European spots just below the very top of the league. City signed Gareth Barry, James Milner and Fabian Delph in a short space of time, and the two clubs went in very different directions. James Milner moved while I was there, leaving for a much larger salary, and the chance of winning trophies, which he certainly did at City, and then Liverpool. As I've mentioned, I took that far too personally.

Later on Milner ended up at Brighton, who are a team that uses a lot of data and analysis and have done very well out of that. They have been good at getting players for relatively little money and selling them on for huge profit: Moisés Caicedo was signed for £4 million and sold to Chelsea for £115 million just a couple of years later. Manchester United were actually linked with Caicedo while he was in Ecuador, and it's easy to say they should have beaten Brighton to him. But it's easier for Brighton to get more of a bargain. If I'm the owner of a club in Ecuador and we've got a good player, there's a certain price for Brighton, and a different one for Manchester United. Also, it's easier at a team like Brighton to get a feel for the Premier League, with less pressure to win matches. If you have a bad performance at Manchester United, the level of noise and pressure is huge, especially since the arrival of social media. Teams like Brighton and Brentford have had a lot of success on a smallish budget, and it feels like everyone's trying to emulate that. But Manchester United can't do exactly the same thing, because they're Manchester United, and the expectations and pressures are completely different.

That does not mean that Brighton and Brentford, having spent a number of successful years in the Premier League, don't have their own ambitions. If I'm a Brighton season ticket holder, I'll want the club to hold on to some of our good players because I want European football and to have a go at winning a trophy. They did really well to get into Europe for the first time for the 2023–24 season, playing against the likes of Marseille and Roma, and spent quite a bit of money the season after that – they are an ambitious club. But, ultimately, they are always going to sell to a club with more money if the price is right. There is nothing wrong with that. I felt that at Leicester we were punching above our weight, which can be an advantage because I was probably able to get players more cheaply than bigger clubs. Not too many clubs would have been after players like Matty Elliott and Muzzy Izzet, but they did really well. Sometimes managing a team like Leicester City can be more rewarding than managing one of the bigger clubs where you're expected to win every week.

A Changing Market

One of the biggest changes to the transfer market happened in 1995 because of a Belgian called Jean-Marc Bosman. He was a fairly obscure player, but his footballing abilities are not the main reason his name is known. He was playing for RFC Liège in Belgium and wanted a transfer to Dunkerque in France. His contract was running out but his club wanted to pay him less money and not let him move. He should have been able to walk away, which is the norm in any other job, but the club were holding on to his registration while offering him less money. It was totally unfair, and Bosman took the club to the European Court of Justice (ECJ). The court agreed with him, issued a ruling saying it went against the European Union's freedom of labour laws, and after that players could simply leave clubs for free when their contracts ran out.

The Bosman ruling has had a huge impact on the game.

Before, football was largely self-governing, but then everything changed. Bosman was absolutely correct in fighting his case, but what was unforeseen at the time was how much the game would shift in the direction of player power. These days when a player has a couple of years left on his contract, he has a lot more bargaining power to ask for higher wages, because the club does not want to lose him for free. Since that legal case, it has been happening more and more often, with points deductions and disqualifications being decided in court rooms rather than on football pitches. Another consequence of the Bosman ruling has been the lifting of quotas on foreign players. In 1995 the Champions League final between Ajax and AC Milan was played almost entirely between Dutch and Italian players. Everything would change in the following years because of Bosman, alongside the growing influence of money at the top of the game, which made football increasingly international over time.

Another new development is the transfer window. When I started out you could transfer to another club until the third week of March. That was for integrity reasons, to stop a club going for the title, signing a bunch of short-term contracts with players from a team with nothing to play for. That would undermine the spirit of the league. But a formal window was introduced in 2002 where teams could only sign players in the summer up until a date at the end of August or start of September, and then again during the month of January. It enabled managers to plan a bit better and not be worried their best player was going to leave suddenly while they were in a relegation fight.

The transfer market has always been competitive, but I think nowadays the level of money that's involved means it is more cut-throat than ever before. Back in my playing days clubs weren't usually dealing with agents, it was club-to-club and manager-to-manager, but that has all changed. The level of money means everybody wants a cut. Often agents are trying to move players on for their own financial interests because it's no good for them if a player stays where he is and signs a nine-year contract. They make money only when players move, so there are always people pushing for transfers. Another shift in the transfer market recently is the obsession with youth. Clubs have always wanted young players, because you can buy them cheaper than the finished product and develop them, but now it is an obsession. As I mentioned in the money chapter, the result is that players are almost treated like financial assets rather than players there to win football matches. This is particularly the case because the sale of academy players is counted as 'pure profit' when it comes to the financial rules, so there is an extra incentive to sell them rather than players who have been signed for a fee. It is increasingly rare for young players from the biggest clubs to come through and play for the first team, which is unfortunate because fans always love to watch 'one of their own' do well. It really doesn't happen often enough these days considering the top clubs have so many young players on their books.

TRANSFERS

I sometimes feel at the moment in football there is too much thinking about the future and not enough about the present. If you lose on a Saturday, nobody will give a fig if the youth team has won some games or if you've signed some bright prospects. There is all this talk of projects and five-year plans, but you have to win football matches or you won't last long. The only way you can influence the whole of a football club is by winning games. It gives you power as a manager. If you win football matches, or end up winning a trophy, that's what matters. Then perhaps you can stamp your authority and personality around the football club if you give it long enough. Without that, a project or long-term plan doesn't mean very much – although, of course, it's good to have a strong academy. I think managers should be empowered to make the transfers that matter, and that, ultimately, seeing a player with your own eyes is the most effective way to find talent.

8

STADIUMS

It was one of the biggest games in Nottingham Forest's history, but the pitch was an absolute bog-heap. The game in question was the European Cup semi-final first leg against Cologne in 1979 at the City Ground, which ended 3–3, before we went to their place and won 1–0 to reach the final. You can watch the extended highlights on YouTube of that first game. It was April, so not the worst time of year for weather, but in those days the pitch used to deteriorate as the season went on. You would start off in August with it looking fantastic, the sun shining and the ball zipping off the turf. That might have been the case for about six or seven weeks before the grim autumn weather came along. By October time, when the clocks change and it is getting dark by the time a Saturday afternoon game is finishing, the pitch would be completely churned up. By the New Year, depending on how bad the winter was, some games could be being played on truly dreadful pitches. Things could get even worse in the spring if there was a lot of rain.

A pitch doesn't deteriorate evenly, as you can see if you watch the footage of that Cologne game. The first area to get churned up is the goalmouth, where lots of players cram in at a corner or a free-kick, scuffing up the grass. The damaged areas spread out like a disease, turning the green penalty box brown, the mud slowly spreading across the rest of the pitch. Eventually you would only see a spot of green in the corners where the ball seldom travels. This is a sight you will never see in a professional football stadium any more. When I look back on my time in the game, it is immediately apparent how the visual architecture of the game – stadiums, training grounds, dressing rooms – has changed immensely.

Pitches and Changing Rooms

These days all sorts of technology ensures football pitches stay green throughout the year. The top stadiums have undersoil heating, and so do plenty of grounds even quite far down the football pyramid. The technology existed in some grounds during my playing career but it was far more primitive. You wouldn't believe some of the pitches in my day. We played on actual snow, and on icy pitches, where you had to wear moulded rubber studs rather than long metal ones in order to keep your balance, or you would be slipping and sliding all over the place. It was crazy looking back on it. Even though the pitches were often awful, it was rare that games were postponed or abandoned, even if the pitch was terrible and you could barely string two passes together. Generally, a game would only be called off if the pitch was completely waterlogged with huge puddles everywhere, meaning the ball couldn't roll at all. But that was uncommon. The referees and everybody else would do everything they could to allow the game to go ahead, and a lot of matches, even at the very top level, were played on bog-heaps like the City Ground for that huge game against Cologne.

The pitches influenced the style of play a lot. Graeme Souness, a midfielder for the excellent Liverpool team of the 1970s and 1980s, was very good with the ball at his feet, for instance. But a lot of the pitches back then were very bobbly and muddy, and the ball would get stuck underneath your feet. In a way there is more skill in doing that than in dealing with the ball on a perfect modern pitch. Also, because all players were less fit then – that's just a fact, in the same way running times have got a lot quicker over time – defenders relied more on positioning and using their heads instead of their feet. Of course, the modern defenders have to be very smart too, and lots of them are, but it was just a slightly different game back then.

For a while in the 1970s some clubs played on Astroturf pitches. They were terrible. They fared better in the winter than grass did, which was the point, but it was like playing on cement. Loftus Road, the home of Queens Park Rangers, had an infamous plastic pitch. You could barely play football there because the ball would be bouncing around all over the place. Luton, Preston and Oldham also had plastic pitches for a while.

When I was managing in Scotland, Dunfermline brought one in for two seasons. I didn't like it at all: it was like an ice rink, and I worried about my players picking up an injury. In Scotland, where the winters are generally harsher and longer than in England and grass pitches are more likely to deteriorate, plastic pitches have appeared over the years. I can see why part-time or amateur clubs like them, because it's good for everyday use. You can have kids' teams and other events during the week, which you can't do with a grass pitch as it will get worn out. But I just think it is not acceptable at the top level – the game you play on a plastic pitch is just not football, and it can be actively dangerous if players are not used to it. I'd always rather play on a boggy pitch than a plastic one. The football boots players wear these days are much lighter, so it is a lot easier for players to turn their ankles. After my time in Scotland, Kilmarnock and Livingston had artificial pitches, but in 2024 the Scottish Premiership rightly banned them. Another reason I dislike them is I think it gives an advantage to teams that are used to it. While at Aston Villa, we played CSKA Moscow on a plastic pitch in the UEFA Cup. I was worried about injuries and it didn't seem fair that they were used to the surface but we were not. There have been some international games played on them, like in the Faroe Islands, which is perhaps more understandable given the weather there. Young Boys in Switzerland have had a plastic pitch in the Champions League in recent years. They still exist but I really don't like them in general.

At the top clubs, the pitch technology is so much more

advanced now. Even in the last five or ten years I have noticed really big improvements. At the Tottenham Hotspur Stadium the pitch can be rolled up and replaced with a pitch for American football. The people who look after all this are very talented and constantly discovering new things. I had an excellent groundsman at Aston Villa, a fellow Northern Irishman called Jonathan Calderwood. He impressed Gerard Houllier, my successor as Villa boss, and was headhunted by Paris Saint-Germain after Houllier gave him a glowing reference – he was still doing that job in 2025 when they won the Champions League. Most major stadiums these days use a technology called GrassMaster, which used to be known as Desso, after the company that made the surface. It is a bit like a plastic mesh with real grass growing through, and it makes pitches much more hardwearing than if they were grass only, without the downsides presented by fully artificial pitches. Even in the depths of winter they generally look pretty good. In winter you can have lights come on to encourage growth, which is useful if a pitch is getting a bit worn out.

As a manager I would always be very aware of the pitch situation at my home stadium because it affects the way you play. The big issue always used to be mud, but with improved technology you can now get the opposite issue of a pitch being too hard. You don't want that because it makes it harder to control the ball and makes injuries more likely. In my early days at Aston Villa I thought the pitch was too hard and the ball was bouncing around all over the place, so I spoke to the ground staff and they helped me get the pitch the way I wanted it. The number of staff dealing with this stuff at any club has increased hugely. Not so long ago it would have just been one groundsman, but now there tends to be a whole army of staff. I used to speak to the ground staff a lot at Celtic because Glasgow winters are very wet, which puts a lot of strain on the pitch. They did a really great job. If the weather was getting bad they would lay down some plastic sheeting to keep the surface drier, but if the temperatures were going to seriously drop there wasn't a lot you could do about the pitch freezing.

Facilities have improved a lot because football clubs have far more money than they used to, thanks mainly to the broadcast deals. Even in the last ten years or so there has been a really big shift in training facilities. When I was managing Villa, an established Premier League team with decent money behind us, the training facilities were quite basic compared to what would come a decade or two later. I went to Manchester City a couple of years ago and saw their training facilities. They are absolutely terrific: there are indoor domes with perfect grass. I went to Leicester City's too, a club with far less money than Man City, and it was incredible compared to what I had at the same club a couple of decades earlier. At both clubs, as well as the indoor facilities there were so many outdoor pitches, with so many groundsmen working on them. My only slight criticism of these modern training grounds is that they are so big that they can feel a bit impersonal. Maybe that's just a consequence of the modern game, but I feel some of these places have lost that personal touch, and maybe that rubs off on the players a little bit, making it harder for them to bond with their club. It's important to know the people who work at the training ground – not just the players and coaches but also the staff, who are really important people.

The facilities in a typical stadium have improved hugely. Take dressing rooms. In my early days at Nottingham Forest we would have two or three showers and a communal bath. We all jumped into the bath together, which was the done thing because we had seen other players do it on TV – especially on FA Cup final day when the victors would take the trophy into the communal bath at Wembley. This has all improved and there are more showers now. Dressing rooms have improved, but because there are so many more players and staff, they sometimes feel more cramped. I don't think anyone foresaw the fact that you would have eight, nine or ten subs, and so many non-playing staff. Dressing rooms have had to expand where they can, but some football clubs, even in the Premier League, have found that difficult. I was at Forest in 2019, and we had more players than teams in the past. The City Ground is an old stadium where it's not that easy to change things a lot, and it was certainly cramped. New stadiums, like Tottenham Hotspur's, are phenomenal in the sense of more space. One thing I can't understand is the modern day development of having lots of staff mingling around listening to your team talk, far more so than would have been the case in my time. Under Brian Clough, you might have had the physiotherapist but he was probably in the other room. I think it made the players more focused. You don't want a dressing room to be too big. With Ireland we used to play at the Aviva Stadium, which is used for rugby, a sport with more players and bigger players. There was too much room. You want something a bit more intimate. You want to try to get the players focused into a corner where they will really listen to your message, rather than have them all spread across a huge area.

Stadium Memories

Grounds used to be volatile, even dangerous places in the fairly recent past. The game in England was closely associated with hooliganism, a long way from the family-friendly day out it would become a few decades later. There is one time in my career I felt really worried for my safety, alongside that trip to Ankara in Turkey with Northern Ireland I mentioned in chapter 2. Forest were playing Newcastle away in the quarter-final of the FA Cup in 1974. The crowd invaded the pitch and it really felt dangerous. I am lucky that these are the only experiences that really stick in my mind. I was recently watching some footage of the 1987 FA Cup final between Tottenham and Coventry, and towards the end of the match the crowd came on to the pitch. There were boys charging all over the place and the game was stopped. The culture surrounding football was very different in the 1980s, and many people got hurt or even killed, most famously at an FA Cup semi-final at Hillsborough, where 97 Liverpool fans ended up losing their lives at a game against Nottingham Forest, a few years after I had left the club. Nobody should ever go to a football match and not come home alive. The core reason for the deaths at Hillsborough was the wire fences which had gone up in response to earlier crowd trouble, and which became extremely dangerous in a crush. A crush killed 66 at Ibrox in 1971, and 56 died in a fire at Bradford's Valley Parade in 1985, which occurred just a few weeks before the Heysel Stadium disaster in Belgium where 39 died. Far too many people lost their lives going to football matches, and the game was seen as something pretty unsavoury – very different to what it is like now. At the time it didn't feel like the game I wanted it to be, with fans watching through fences, hooligans marauding outside grounds, and very few women and children in the crowd.

After Hillsborough there was the Taylor Report, which recommended all-seater stadiums, and lots of English grounds were rebuilt in the early 1990s as a result. This didn't happen abroad, and clubs like Dortmund in Germany kept their huge terraces where the hardcore supporters stood. The move to all-seater stadiums changed footballing culture, and I do think something was lost with all that, although it's understandable that it happened in the aftermath of Hillsborough. There has been a recognition in recent times that standing at football, which is a positive thing, can be made safe. The authorities have reintroduced standing for a minority of fans that want it inside plenty of English grounds, which is pleasing to see. People generally make a lot more noise when they're standing up rather than sitting down and it is good for the atmosphere of a stadium. This is so-called 'rail seating', where there is a rail in between each row, which significantly lessens the risk of the crushes that happened on the old terraces, and, of course, there are none of those horrible wire fences between the fans and the pitch now.

Speaking of the unpleasant side of football culture and how it has changed, racism was very common in my playing days. I was the right-winger for Nottingham Forest, and Viv Anderson, the first Black player to play for England, was the right-back. That meant two of us were generally getting abused by the crowd on the same side of the pitch. We used to joke to each other that we would fight over who wanted to take a throw-in. Being Northern Irish, with the political situation at the time, I would get a lot of stick from opposition fans, while Viv would get racist abuse. It was completely unacceptable and there is far less of it now, which is a very good thing. Of course, the issue has not gone away, and lots of it has moved from the terraces to social media. There was an acceptance of it back then and a feeling that players should just get on with it, but that should never have been the case. It wasn't just a case of one person shouting something obnoxious in the crowd. Hooligans were organised, and there would be gangs who were using football to have a punch-up or abuse people. Some of that hooliganism might look glamorous in films but it really was not pleasant at the time. Millwall was a particularly hostile place. I played a game for Nottingham Forest at the Old Den and our bus was stoned on the way in and again on the way out. I remember a window being broken and it was very intimidating. At Forest in the 1970s we used to have a pre-match meal before home games at the Bridgford Hotel on the corner of Trent Bridge, and would be sitting by the windows on the sixth or seventh floor watching the fans down below. You could see the away fans coming from the train station over the bridge, where they would be met by our fans and just fight in the street. We would watch it while having our pre-game lunch, almost like entertainment. The police would be trying their best but little skirmishes would be taking place, and then those skirmishes became bigger. It was almost just taken for granted that people would go to the football and have a scrap.

All stadiums have different characters and crowds and that affects the game you play. My favourite ground to visit was always Ibrox for the Old Firm games. It was really hostile but I didn't mind that aspect of it: the intensity of that rivalry is a special thing. You would have about ten or 15 yards to cover between the bus and the stadium entrance and you would get the dog's abuse. It wasn't pleasant at the time, but there was something good about it because it showed how much supporting their team matters to people. The Rangers manager would face the same reception at Celtic Park. We were fierce rivals but I had great regard for the Rangers fans, for Ibrox and the football club in general. It's unfortunate that recent Old Firm games between Celtic and Rangers have had no away fans, or very few of them. In my time there as a manager you had maybe 6,000 or 7,000 away fans in the stadium. I think the change started because Rangers were losing so often that they decided to take the Celtic fans out of Ibrox. Once you do that the same thing is inevitably going to happen at the other place. It would be lovely to see 6,000 or 7,000 Celtic fans at Ibrox again, and the same number of Rangers fans at Celtic Park – it can create an incredible atmosphere at an Old Firm game. Because so many of the other domestic games are quite predictable, it means the intensity of those games is something else. You might expect there to be lots of trouble but it's always a very early kick-off time, and there are lots of police, so it's generally OK.

There's nothing quite like those matches in world football, especially at the time I was there when both teams had a lot of great players and were closely matched. In my first season there we hadn't had a win at Ibrox for six-and-a-half years, then we went and won 3–0 with two goals from Lubo Moravčík and one from Henrik Larsson. That was a very special day. We had already won the league but I got into a bit of trouble as I was getting the dog's abuse coming off the bus because I just said the word, 'Champions,' to the fans. They didn't like that! At one point we beat them seven games in a row, which is still a record. Thinking back, those Old Firm days are some of my happiest memories in football, especially the wins at Ibrox. It was a big challenge quietening that hostile crowd but I managed it plenty of times!

Aston Villa versus Birmingham City was a pretty fierce rivalry too. Just before my time there some of those games got pretty ugly. Birmingham had been in the lower divisions for years, so the two teams hadn't played each other for a very long time and crowd trouble really boiled over at a couple of weekday evening games. Kick-off time does make a big difference to that sort of thing. The earlier the game, the less time there is for people to get drunk. When they switched that fixture to weekend lunchtime kick-offs it was generally OK. I played Birmingham four times during my spell at Villa and had a perfect record against them, with four wins including a 5–1 which was very enjoyable indeed.

The most atmospheric ground that I have ever played in was Anfield, both as a player and as a manager. I look back to some of the massive battles we had there when I was at Nottingham Forest. The one that mattered most was the one in 1978 in the first round of the European Cup. We weren't sure if our 2–0 lead from the City Ground would be enough at Anfield, but we put in an amazing performance to draw 0–0. Another great Anfield memory was when I went there with Celtic in the quarter-final of the UEFA Cup the season we got to the final. We beat them 2–0 in the second leg after drawing at our place. Celtic players tell me my team talk was really motivational, although I don't remember exactly what I said. I also enjoyed winning 2–1 there with Leicester City in August 1997. It was the start of our second season in the Premier League, a few months after we'd won the League Cup and finished ninth, so we were on a real high at that point.

I found the most hostile ground to be the one on the other side of Stanley Park – Goodison Park, which was Everton's home until 2025, when they moved into a brand new stadium at Bramley-Moore Dock, a couple of miles away. There's an old cliché that managers always come out with before an away game: 'Let's keep the home crowd quiet for the first 20 minutes.' Goodison was definitely one place where that applied: the crowd could get on the backs of their own players pretty quickly. When they were buzzing and upbeat, though, things could get really hostile for the opposing team. The linesman on the far side would be stricken with fear. Before VAR came in they would have their hand up in the air for offside because the crowd behind them was shouting at them, even if it looked onside. I had a special win there in 2008 with Aston Villa. Everton equalised in the very last minute to make it 2–2, but then Ashley Young immediately went down the other end and scored the winner. There is no feeling quite like a last-minute winner, especially when you've just had the agony of conceding an equaliser from what you thought was the last kick of the game. Ashley Young was 23 then – I couldn't have imagined he would be playing at the same stadium for Everton 17 years later.

Old Trafford is always a great place to go as well. It's impossible not to think of the history of the club, with George Best's time there very special to me as a Northern Irishman too, of course.

The team has struggled recently but Manchester United are still Manchester United, and it is still an amazing place. One game stands out in my memory from all the many times I have been there as a player then a manager. It was January 1998, I was Leicester manager and United were the reigning champions whereas we were still relatively new kids on the block. We started off defending well, then in the 30th minute Garry Parker clipped the ball into the box and it bounced kindly for Tony Cottee who hit it past Peter Schmeichel. Our away fans went mad. We somehow kept it to 1–0. Our keeper Kasey Keller was brilliant that day. A lot of teams have won at Old Trafford since Sir Alex Ferguson left, but back then it was a momentous achievement for a team like Leicester. It's a great feeling shutting up 70,000 people like that. Of course, lots of other times I didn't get such a good result there, but it was always a special place to go.

I have been to plenty of iconic stadiums overseas as well, and got some decent results. I managed Celtic in the Nou Camp twice and got a draw both times. In the UEFA Cup we beat them 1–0 at home so we knocked them out. That was just before the era of Guardiola and Messi, although they still had some fantastic players: Xavi, Ronaldinho and Carles Puyol. Shutting them out 0–0 at the Nou Camp is one of my favourite football memories; it is always so much harder playing away from home in Europe, with all the travel, the unfamiliar surroundings and the crowd.

Another hostile place in Spain is Valencia's Mestalla

Stadium. It was there I played for Northern Ireland in the group stages of the 1982 World Cup against Spain, the hosts, and the atmosphere was very intimidating. I was captain and we were playing in our first World Cup for 24 years. They had a very good team, so we were huge underdogs. We knew that even though they were favourites, we would surely get one chance, and it came just after half-time. The ball fell to Gerry Armstrong from a cross and he made no mistake. It felt like the referee was very favourable to the home team, and that every decision that he made in favour of us – which was not many – was hotly disputed by the players and the crowd. He sent our defender Mal Donaghy off with 30 minutes to go. I'm not sure the referee had seen the incident; he just came up and gave him a card, which he should never have done. You felt that every single time a Spanish player went down in the penalty area, the Argentinian ref might just blow for a penalty. But we somehow got through the game without conceding, and he never pointed to the penalty spot. Maybe the sending off helped with that. Referees always try to say that all decisions are independent from each other, and that if they give a penalty for or against you they're no more or less likely to give a red card, but I don't think that's ever quite true. That Spain result was magical. We had drawn with Honduras and Yugoslavia, so nobody gave us much hope of getting through, but the Spain win meant we came top of our group. We ended up going out after losing 4–1 to France in Madrid, but we were very proud of what we achieved.

For very different reasons, I was always a big fan of the old Juventus stadium, the Stadio Delle Alpi. It was apparently an unpleasant place for fans to go, with poor facilities. But the thing I liked about that place is it had a huge running track around it, which was good for the away side as it meant the atmosphere was terrible. You would far rather play somewhere like that than in front of a noisy hostile crowd who are close to the pitch. The crowds there were surprisingly poor despite Juventus being the best-supported club in Italy. The club tore it down and built a new, more compact venue on the same site in 2011, now called the Allianz Stadium, where the crowd is much closer to the action. Quite a lot of Italian teams in particular have stadiums with running tracks, which means there is just no atmosphere. West Ham have struggled a bit with the London Stadium, which was built to host the 2012 Olympics. They have taken out the running track but the stands are shallow rather than steep, which means a lot of the fans are far from the action. It's not as good as some of the other modern stadiums like Arsenal's and especially Tottenham's where the fans are closer to the pitch.

The Role of a Stadium

There was actually very little change in English football stadiums before the Second World War – in fact, right up until the 1990s. But there's been a huge amount of change since then, which has been good for the most part, although it's always sad when an old ground closes its doors. The Tottenham Hotspur Stadium is a fantastic football ground, and I like that it's been built on the same spot as the old White Hart Lane. Everton have moved a couple of miles towards the Mersey, and I'm sure that in 100 years' time Bramley-Moore Dock will have its own history, just like Goodison did, although a new stadium is inevitably a bit strange at the very beginning when everything is a bit too clean and shiny and holds no memories yet. Arsenal's old stadium at Highbury, which they left in 2006, was a special place. It was hidden away in the dense residential streets of north London, and when you walked in there was a marble hall furnished with busts of some of the greats of the past like Herbert Chapman. If I had owned the club I would have loved to have built the new place on the exact spot – but that wasn't to be as it is penned in by housing. The Emirates is very close by, though. The new stadium is a lot bigger, and they make a lot more money from it. That's called progress – the world moves on, and change is necessary sometimes. Liverpool tried something different in expanding their existing stadium rather than moving, which they had planned to do at various points in time, but the Anfield upgrades have been positive and they have increased capacity without the need for a new location. West Ham's old ground of Upton Park was really special. I miss it, alongside Highbury, Goodison Park and perhaps most of all Roker Park, which was for a long time the home of Sunderland, and in the north-east there was also Middlesbrough's Ayresome Park. Those two were replaced in the 1990s by the Stadium of Light and the Riverside Stadium, the first new big all-seater stadiums in England for a long time. They are good in their own way, but it's hard not to be nostalgic.

Today, lots of clubs have plans to expand or move because tickets are increasingly in demand, and there is a lot of pressure to make more money from things like corporate hospitality. If people want to sit down and have something to eat before a match, there's no problem with that. I've done it a bit, mainly at Tottenham and Arsenal. I enjoyed it, but I don't want to be one of those people who goes to a former club and shakes people's hands each week. That's not for me, although I have been back to Wycombe quite a few times.

A modern football stadium seems geared towards how the game looks on TV – it caters for that just as much as it does for the people who experience the game in the ground. Modern football at the top level is often about creating a broadcast product rather than a game to be experienced live. Again, that's no bad thing – I watch an awful lot of football on TV – but it can't be the main thing. There is something about a match in such an environment that's missing but I can't quite put my finger on it. The product is still very strong, as it has to be because the broadcasters are paying a lot of money for it. The top players are still a joy to watch, there's no question about that. But the amount of money the matchday experience costs these days is troubling to me. Still, plenty of people are willing to pay to go and watch football. It is easy to be nostalgic about the past, but match attendances have been really strong in England in recent years, even way down the football pyramid. People are voting with their feet and far more people are going to live games than in the 1980s. It's a good thing, and an example of football improving, though I do worry about the future if prices keep going up.

As well as the stadiums themselves, the general experience of playing a top-level match has changed a lot over the past few decades, as clubs have got richer. When we travelled as a team in my playing days we always shared a room with somebody back then, which isn't the case now. But back then that extra money mattered a lot more to the club. My roommate on trips away would often be Viv Anderson or John Robertson. Sometimes you would be allowed to keep the same partner, then at times they mixed them up, just to change it around a bit. The club would want everyone to rub along with each other, rather than cliques forming. Generally with Nottingham Forest if we were staying overnight before an away game we would tend to go for a walk as a group at around 11 o'clock in the morning before the match. If it was a hotel that had grounds that would work nicely, or if it was a hotel in London we'd often walk around the centre of town, sometimes even around Charing Cross right in the middle of London, which probably wouldn't happen now. There would be lots of people coming up to us, especially when I was in the Forest team that was winning lots of trophies and was becoming really well known. These days somebody would film that and put it on social media, and the next thing you know there would be a mob, or maybe rival fans being unpleasant, or something. You did get attention from the public, but because nobody knew about it in advance it was generally OK.

9

MANAGERS

We have already spent a lot of time here talking about the role of a manager, but it deserves its own chapter because the manager is the most important person in any football club – or at least I'd like to think that is still the case. In my playing days the manager was a dominant figure, and there weren't too many other full-time non-playing staff around at all. But, as already noted, that has changed a lot. A football club is a big business, with lots of people on the payroll now. That means it is more professionally run, and that is a good thing, but sometimes with so many bodies you can lose sight of what really matters above all else – winning football matches, and that is on the manager more than anyone else.

When I look back at all the managers I have worked with, both as a player and as a manager myself, three names come to mind who are perhaps not as well known as some of the ones that came along later. First, I think back to a knock on our door, September 1970, in Troubles-torn Belfast. My mother opens it, staring at a complete stranger who introduces himself. His name is Jimmy McAlinden and he is the manager of Irish league club Distillery. He has made the journey across the city and has made it his business to talk to my parents, and obviously me as well, about signing me for his football club. We have never met before but in the next 12 months he will have a transformative influence in my life. I don't believe he was ever asked how he got our address but I am pleased he made the personal effort to do so.

McAlinden is the first football manager I played for, and it is not too much of a stretch to think he ranks alongside Dave Mackay and Brian Clough as one of the biggest influences on my club football career. He was a brilliant footballer, plying his trade in the English league and winning the FA Cup with Portsmouth in 1939, months before Hitler invaded Poland and started the Second World War. There would not be another FA Cup final until 1946.

The call of home was strong and at the end of his playing career he found himself back in his beloved country. By the time we met he had established himself as a super football manager with a very astute brain – a potent tactical master, and perhaps above all a magnificent motivator. He had assembled at Grosvenor Park, home of Distillery FC, a very fine team who were capable of beating any team in the league on any given day but were perhaps not consistent enough over a season to win the league. This is what he wanted to rectify, he told me, and he believed that I, a mere novice, could help him do that. Regardless of whether he meant that or not, it was an enormous boost to my confidence and even when I met my more established teammates who have already made names for themselves in the Irish league, I did not feel intimidated. Well, perhaps just a little.

For the next 12 months Jimmy took us on a wonderful footballing journey, taking the club into European football by winning the Irish Cup. His personality percolated the club – a common feature among all the great managers I was fortunate enough to work with. The respect he received from the players never wavered, even if there was a dip in results. He could criticise strongly in the dressing room but knew exactly when to row back when he felt his point had been made. He was, to coin a phrase, a players' manager. I personally felt that he would always be on my side if I could live up to his expectations of me. Because to him, regardless of what was going on at boardroom level, he would be in the players' corner if sides had to be taken.

A year on, with a goal against Barcelona and a 20-minute senior international cap to my credit, I became a fully-fledged professional footballer with Nottingham Forest. My second manager was Matt Gillies, a Scotsman who'd had a very successful managerial period at Leicester City some years earlier. Erudite and lucid, Matt exuded a quiet confidence, but beneath the exterior one felt a certain anxiety which would manifest from time to time – and, of course, why wouldn't there be anxiety? Nottingham Forest, the team he was managing, were in the throes of a very poor season and by the end of October 1971 were gripping precariously on to the bottom of the table. Some of his senior players, with the exception of the brilliant Ian

Storey-Moore, were playing poorly and seemingly couldn't get out of the rut. As a £15,000 transfer I don't think he was expecting too much of me.

It was interesting to compare and contrast the two characters that were shaping my footballing career. Both knew the game inside out, both knew the players' characters they were dealing with, but Matt's anxiety would show with each defeat. His job was on the line. In truth, he never blamed individual players publicly for those defeats but he was a troubled man in the dressing room. Not being able to find a consistent winning formula plays constantly on your mind, confidence and motivational ability. Matt, of course, was a manager in the big league where results mattered most. There was no hiding place.

Nottingham Forest were relegated in May 1972 but Matt did not lose his job immediately. He was given the opportunity to get Forest back into the big league, the First Division, but got sacked in October when results in the Second Division were not going down well with the board, and particularly with the supporters. And so, a gentleman of the game, if that is not a contradiction in terms, left football not to work again. I met Matt only one more time after he left Nottingham Forest just to thank him for signing me and putting me on a football career path. He was not bitter, just disappointed in the manner of his departure, but the game had taken its toll and he had seemingly given up the fight. He died a few years later in his Nottingham home.

Third, Dave Mackay was a different character completely. Not the tallest of men, but a man with a big presence nonetheless. If I could come back in another life I would want to be Dave Mackay. A fearless combatant as a player, and wonderfully gifted to boot, he carried that fearlessness and courage, both physical and moral, into management, made the game so simple so anyone could understand him, was better technically than he gave himself credit for, and a leader of men, prepared to listen to the viewpoints of players but deep down was steadfast in his convictions. You played to please him because his praise was worth having.

And then, of course, came Brian Clough, who has to rank among the greatest to ever ply the trade.

The Best Managers

Historically, the very best managers have grasped the importance of winning football matches, with everything else secondary to that. It is always difficult to say who the greatest managers are because you have to judge them according to the era they're working in, and the teams they came up against. From my early days watching football as a child, one name that jumps out is Matt Busby at Manchester United. He was on the plane that crashed on the runway in Munich in 1958, killing lots of players in an excellent young team. He pulled through that tragedy and a decade later won the European Cup; a phenomenal achievement. He might not have been a tactician like many managers are now, but he certainly would have been a man-manager, which you always felt was the main job – you can only imagine the man-management skills involved in not just picking a team up after an event like that, but then also winning the biggest prize in club football. A star of that team was George Best, who was very difficult to deal with in many aspects, but the one person he had enormous respect for was Matt Busby. That is one of the skills of top managers – earning the respect of the very best players, and getting them to play well.

I think Jock Stein's achievement with Celtic was particularly incredible. He won the European Cup in 1967 with a team all born within 30 miles of Glasgow. That will simply never happen again. It's an example of doing incredible things with the tools at your disposal rather than just going out and buying the best players. Of course, the world has changed in that respect, and, as I've noted, football is better for it in many ways, but the legacy of that achievement was always present in my time at Celtic. Another name that jumps out is Bill Shankly at Liverpool who won so many trophies and kickstarted Liverpool's ascent to the top of the English and European game. Before him the club had only won one title in 36 years, but from Shankly onwards they dominated English football for a long time. He was followed by Bob Paisley, who was less of a big presence but ended up winning even more than Shankly, including becoming the first manager to win three European Cups, alongside six league titles. Then, of course, there was Brian Clough, my own manager for so long. Given all his achievements in the game – getting Forest promoted, winning the league at the City Ground, having also won it at Derby, as well as the European Cup twice – he would have to be in any conversation to be one of the greatest managers of all time, especially considering where Forest started and where they ended up. You're judging all these names by the era they managed in. Everything has changed so much. Would Busby or Clough struggle in the modern game? Who knows. Maybe the best modern managers might have struggled in bygone epochs. The skills you need have changed a lot over time.

In the modern game one of the greats is Pep Guardiola, there is no question about that. What he's done at Manchester City has been fantastic. He has obviously been aided greatly by the amount of money that he's been given but, even so, you only have to look to the other side of Manchester to see another team that has spent an awful lot of money and not been anywhere near as good in recent years. Guardiola has played a huge part in City winning so many trophies. I would put Jürgen Klopp in the conversation as well when it comes to the modern greats – for his successes not just with Liverpool but in Germany, winning the league with Dortmund. Winning the league there is always a huge achievement for any club that isn't Bayern Munich. Klopp was perhaps a little unlucky to only win the Premier League once given how good his team was, coming up against Manchester City at the peak of their powers, twice missing out on the title by just a point. Still, they won the Champions League and everything there is to win domestically. Jürgen Klopp is a top, top manager.

As I think about who is the best manager of all-time, though – with all the caveats about comparing different people across eras – I keep coming back to one name: Sir Alex Ferguson. The thing that makes him stand out to me is his longevity; managing Manchester United from 1986 to 2013. This is a book about how football has changed over time, from a simpler game before the Premier League and big money came along to the game we know today, with all its flaws and brilliance. Ferguson's career essentially straddled that divide and he adapted to incredibly different eras. There were 23 years between his first and last trophies at Manchester United, and 27 between his first and last games. In his first season Ferguson managed Frank Stapleton, who was born in 1956, two years before the Munich air crash. In his last season his starting goalkeeper was David de Gea, born in 1990, and even younger players like Jesse Lingard and Phil Jones were on the fringes of that squad. In between, of course, you had so many huge names, from Bryan Robson to Robin van Persie, with Peter Schmeichel, Eric Cantona, Ryan Giggs, Roy Keane, Paul Scholes, David Beckham, Ruud van Nistelrooy, Rio Ferdinand, Cristiano Ronaldo, Wayne Rooney and so many others in between.

I can't think of anyone who comes close to replicating that achievement, especially at one club, where there is always a danger of things going stale and players no longer listening to you if you stay too long. It's easy to forget that after three years at Old Trafford he was unpopular and there were banners saying 'Ferguson Out'. How wrong could one be? He admits himself that some players at the time were signed to try to get them out of the relegation spots, but, of course, his team went on to become completely dominant, winning 13 of the first 21 Premier League titles, and the European Cup twice, as well as countless other honours. I don't pretend to know him well but, like everyone else in the game, have undiluted respect for his achievements.

Thinking about other managers from the Premier League – a rung below Ferguson for me but still hugely impressive – Arsène Wenger would have to be up there when we're considering people who changed the game in England; he is a very significant figure, in embracing foreign players and new ways of doing things, such as seeing the importance of diet and nutrition before many others in England did. José Mourinho has been a fantastic manager too, winning the Champions League with Porto (then again later with Inter Milan) and then coming to England with Chelsea and winning the league in his first two seasons, as well as many other trophies. An incredible achievement in breaking up the Manchester United and Arsenal 'Big Two' as it was back then. Mourinho teams were so solid defensively, but with playmakers to win games. In the 2004–05 season they conceded just 15 goals. I'm not sure that will ever be repeated – the Premier League is higher scoring than it was back then and there is more focus on attacking football. I wouldn't be surprised if that achievement is still standing in 100 years.

Looking outside the UK, another top manager who I came up against a number of times is Carlo Ancelotti. We were drawn against his AC Milan side in the 2004–05 Champions League group stages. We lost 3–1 in Italy but ground out a 0–0 draw at Celtic Park – a good result that unfortunately wasn't enough to stop us going out of Europe. We had so many chances that day, it was very frustrating. That was the year they lost the Champions League final on penalties following Liverpool's spectacular comeback in Istanbul, but two years later he managed to get revenge against the same opposition in the Champions League final in Athens. Ancelotti has always struck me as very calm, and not one to let a defeat ruin too much: he just moves on to the next game, and generally wins it. He is also someone whose achievements have spanned a long period of time, winning the Champions League with AC Milan in 2003 and 2007, and then three times with Real Madrid, first in 2014, before he left and came back years later to win it in 2022 and 2024. That is not even to mention all the domestic honours he has won, including league titles in the 'Big Five' leagues of Spain, Italy, France, Germany and England, the only person to manage that. His record speaks for itself – he has won more Champions Leagues as manager than anyone else, as well as two as a player with AC Milan. In 2025 he became manager of Brazil, his first taste of international management.

I came up against Ancelotti three times when he was at Chelsea and I was at Villa. A few weeks after we lost the League Cup final in 2010, we went to Stamford Bridge and lost 7–1, with Frank Lampard getting a hat-trick. The less said about that the better. Two weeks later we lost the FA Cup semi-final 3–0 to them. We played quite well in that game and should have had a penalty early on, but that was a rough few weeks. The one I prefer to remember was when we beat Chelsea 2–1 at Villa Park in the league in October 2009, not long after he had joined. James Collins headed the winner from a corner, which was his first goal in four years. I have a funny memory about Ancelotti from that game. My assistant John Robertson always liked to smoke before a match, and as he was doing so, about 35 minutes before kick-off as the ground was filling up, he got a tap on the shoulder. It was Ancelotti having a smoke as well. Changes in the smoking laws mean you can't light up so close to the dressing room now. You sometimes see Ancelotti with a vape on the touchline, though. He didn't let that defeat affect his team too badly – they won the league and cup double that season, but he got sacked the next year after coming second. Roman Abramovich has said that sacking him was his biggest mistake.

Another top manager that comes to mind is Giovanni Trapattoni, who won the league in four different countries and a UEFA Cup with Inter, and is well known to me because he managed Ireland immediately before I did. He was desperately unlucky not to qualify for the World Cup in 2010 because of Thierry Henry's famous handball, which didn't get spotted by the officials when he scored the goal that knocked Ireland out, which was a terrible refereeing error. Another Italian I have huge admiration for is Claudio Ranieri, who won the Premier League with Leicester City in 2015–16, one of the most incredible achievements in the history of sport. After that he had a tough time of things and was sacked by Fulham and then Watford, which was quite a climb-down. But he went back to Cagliari and got them promoted, then ended up at Roma, one of the biggest clubs in Europe, at the age of 73, and performed brilliantly with them in his last season, dragging them from the relegation zone to European qualification.

The role of the manager can vary between countries. Italian football seems to be much more forgiving in a way, so if you have a job that doesn't go so well, people are less quick to completely write you off, and accept that sometimes you can be the right man at the wrong time. Another interesting thing about Italian football is that all the top managers – Ancelotti, Antonio Conte, Marcello Lippi, Trapattoni, Fabio Capello – have managed multiple big clubs in Italy. That doesn't really happen in England, for whatever reason. I think the culture is more transactional over there, and managers often don't stay in a job for long, whereas in England if you go from Liverpool to Manchester United it's seen as a huge betrayal. Most of the top English clubs have had one or two managers who have stayed for a really long time.

But that is not the only way to run a successful football club. Real Madrid and Bayern Munich are two huge teams that tend to keep managers for two or three years before changing things up. Neither club has a Sir Alex Ferguson equivalent. Perhaps there's the sense that the club is always bigger than any one manager. The standards are so high that you are expected to win titles every year – the league or the Champions League – and if you don't you move on. Chelsea under Abramovich had that model, never holding on to a manager for very long, whereas other English clubs have had long-term managers: Ferguson, Wenger, Klopp, Guardiola. It's interesting that the longest managerial stints in England often occur at the biggest clubs. Things are very different lower down the football league where you're fighting for survival or for promotion. A 'new manager bounce' – getting two or three wins – can mean everything, so chairmen perhaps are more likely to chop and change. The Championship has an amazingly high turnover: often more than half of the managers there have been in a job for less than a year. The prize of success is so great that if things aren't working out, change seems inevitable. At the very top of the game it's harder to believe there are better options out there if you have a bad run.

Tense Contests

'An enterprising contest of chances aplenty but shy of goals,' writes one reporter following Aston Villa's goalless draw with Arsenal at Villa Park on a late January evening in 2010. As Villa manager, I consider this is a fair summary of the evening's encounter. At the end of the game Arsenal's excellent manager,

Arsène Wenger, gives me a cursory glance, his handshake and face going in opposite directions. He is naturally disappointed that his very gifted team, lying third in the Premier League table, have not been able to take all three points and cut Chelsea's lead at the top. I, in turn, am frustrated that we have not made use of the chances we created. The draw, even against such illustrious opponents, thwarts our chances of climbing into a Champions League position. I wish Gabby Agbonlahor had scored from a very early chance, and that Stewart Downing had been able to convert one of the two clear-cut opportunities that had fallen to him, but I take some consolation in that we were always in the game and that victory wasn't far away.

After a dressing-room debrief I am ushered off to the press conference to give my account of the match. Much of what I have just said to the players moments earlier I reiterate to journalists. They allow me to finish my account and although I see a few nods of agreement within the room there are also a number of them who cannot wait to tell me that my version of proceedings differs almost entirely from what the Arsenal manager has just said a few moments ago in this very room. 'What did he say?' I ask, rather quizzically. 'Arsène said that your team was very negative and that long balls were the order of the day. He said that when they come here they know what to expect and, in that respect, they weren't disappointed. You play a very English game.'

I am absolutely furious. These are typical comments from Arsenal's manager after his team couldn't score against us. The journalists also said Arsène had added that we were a counter-attacking team, which on the face of it would seem somewhat of a contradiction if we had already been labelled by him as a long-ball team. I reply that having such players as Ashley Young, James Milner, Stiliyan Petrov, Gabby Agbonlahor and Stewart Downing making up half the team doesn't suggest a long-ball team, at least to me. 'Those pernicious jibes are pretty typical of him,' I remark, and leave the press conference.

A few minutes later I see the Arsenal manager making his way down the corridor heading towards the team bus parked close by outside. I am afraid I cannot let this verbal attack on my team go unremarked upon, so confrontation, certainly on my side, prevails. 'What about your ridiculous comments in the press room?' I say, demanding some sort of answer.

'What comments are you talking about?' he asks, perturbed at my aggressive tone.

'Your usual,' I reply. 'Every team you play against plays a long ball when you don't win. Always your way out.'

'I did not say those things,' he answers.

'So the press are making it up, then?' I retort. 'You should learn to be a little more civil sometimes.' Although as those words come tumbling out there seems to be a little voice in my own head whispering, '*You should be a little more civil yourself, if that's the case.*' 'Just look after your own affairs and don't concern yourself with the opposition, OK?' I blurt out.

As you can imagine, we do not shake hands and he departs with an accusatory stare towards me. I feel better for having said what I did, however fleetingly that feeling will last. My team is packed with terrific footballers. In a few weeks we will contest the League Cup final at Wembley against Sir Alex Ferguson's Manchester United because just last week we got to that hallowed stage by beating Blackburn Rovers 6–4 at Villa Park in one of the most exciting semi-finals in League Cup history.

Four days later I receive a letter in the post watermarked 'Arsenal Football Club'. It is a letter from Arsène himself. I think that, after some quiet introspection, he is going to apologise for the crass comments he made about my team at the press conference. But no, not a bit of it! He is indignant. He chastises me for my rudeness to him and demands an apology from me! I have a wry smile to myself. The press had recounted his comments accurately. Arsenal will go on to finish third in the Premier League, behind Carlo Ancelotti's splendid Chelsea team, and we will qualify for European football by finishing sixth, but tantalisingly out of reach for the Champions League. Perhaps those extra two points for either club on that January evening might have made a difference to the aspirations of Villa or Arsenal. Who knows? For Arsène, despite his penchant for digging at teams that play the 'English Way', has proved himself a brilliant manager, one of the best in Premier League history.

A Manager's Job

Team selection is an obviously important aspect of a head coach's job. Sometimes that is hard, which is what you want: it means you have lots of good players all fighting fit and rivalling each other for a place. You want to play your own game and play to your strengths but you also have to think about the opposition. Naturally you might pick a different line-up and take a different approach in a game where you would expect to dominate the ball compared to one where you'd expect to sit deep and come under a lot of pressure. You would be trying to second-guess what the opposition manager would be doing and remember they always have a plan just as you do. On occasion, my players would give me some intelligence on the opposition. At Aston Villa, Ashley Young or Gabby Agbonlahor were often quite friendly with some of the opposition players and might hear something about their team the night before and be telling me about it. I think they would hear it from players they knew who were frustrated at not being in the team, and, generally speaking, their information was quite accurate! It didn't mean I would make huge adjustments, but if something was going to surprise me and somebody unexpected was going to be playing, then I had all night to think about it and come up with some ideas rather than be scrambling about an hour before the game when the team was announced or, even worse, when you're 2–0 down in the first half.

The assistant manager is a very key figure. Peter Taylor was a huge part of Brian Clough's successes. John Robertson, of course, was for so many years my own assistant, and someone I was very close to. An inspirational footballer and excellent manager himself, Roy Keane accepted the role of assistant manager when I was managing Ireland. Just one generation ahead of those players who would have grown up with reverential respect for him, he espoused strong values within the group. As that old saying goes, he could talk the talk because he could walk the walk. In international football you don't have that many days to work with the squad, so the main focus is getting into players' heads – the motivational side as much as anything else. That was particularly important when we played top sides like Germany and Italy. It was all about getting players to play above themselves at an international level, even if it was only for one game.

Being a manager is all consuming. Also, while the football calendar is relentless and players never get a proper break in a physical sense, they do actually have a lot of downtime in the working week – you can't physically train all day every day, but the manager can fill all the hours in the day with work. Players train in the morning, maybe watch some videos and listen to some talks, get a massage, but it is rarely a long day. It doesn't take anything away from the points I make about fatigue – that is very real – but, as an overall life, players have it pretty good. In management you are always working long days and it is very hard to switch off. I am not complaining – it is the life I chose, and I loved it. But the level of sustained intensity is completely different to being a player, even if it might be less physical work. I didn't have many breaks at all in my career. I barely had a week off from becoming Wycombe manager in 1990 to leaving Celtic in 2005, when I took a year off when my wife was ill – before going back into management at Villa in 2006 where I stayed for four years. After Villa I had about 15 months off before joining Sunderland. I'm not sure what I did all day during that time. I watched a lot of football. I'm not much of a gardener. I was trying to sort some things out that I never had time to when I was a manager. I was glad to get back into it and have eight more years pretty much non-stop, at Sunderland, then Ireland, then Nottingham Forest.

By the end of my time I was really noticing a shift in the role of backroom staff, and, by logical extension, a reduction in the role of the manager. The backroom staff have become so important these days, and managers must cope with that. A manager now must be better at delegating than was the case in my day. I wasn't a good delegator. Obviously, I let the coaches coach, and I let the physio do the physio work, and I let the fitness coach do his thing. But, essentially, in terms of players coming into a football club, as I've outlined, I always wanted to have the final say.

As a manager you want your players to relax and let their hair down. But you can't be letting all that get in the way of the job they are paid very well to do. You had to always be aware of what was going on in players' personal lives. You certainly don't want them getting arrested or anything like that. Your tolerance of things depends hugely on how the player is doing on the pitch, and whether they're showing full commitment.

A manager needs to know the characters and personalities in their team. If someone phoned you and said that something had happened to one of your players last night, you could usually guess who it would be. This would be easier now than it used to be. Technology means everything seems to go straight on the internet these days. It's a lot harder now for players to have a night on the town because they're getting camera phones shoved in their faces. I do think that's a bad thing to an extent, because they should have the right to enjoy themselves occasionally, just like anyone else. There are times when it crosses a line, though, and you find yourself dealing with a tricky situation as a manager.

I took a dim view of my players going out on nights out before big games, but I can look back and laugh about one incident when I was at Aston Villa. My daughter called me early one Friday morning and said, 'Please don't think I'm telling tales, but one of my friends was at a nightclub in London last night and big John Carew was there.' This had been a Thursday night before a Saturday game, and our main striker was in a nightclub at two o'clock in the morning, a couple of hours' drive from the training ground where he was expected the next day. That was completely unacceptable behaviour. I made sure I was waiting for him when he arrived at training and brought him into my office and asked him where he'd been the night before. Of course, he said he'd been at home. I pushed him on that, said he'd been spotted out in a club, but he denied it. I said I had photographic evidence from the nightclub, which I didn't, but then he admitted it in the end. I said I would fine him two weeks' wages but still play him the next day because he was in good form. Anyway, he went and scored and we won the game. John was so popular with the dressing room and the crowd, and after the game he knocked on my door and asked me for a word. He asked me if I thought he'd played well. I said yes, just as I had told him in front of everyone in the dressing room. He then wondered if he could get off the fine. We came to a compromise to fine him only one week's wages, and he was actually delighted with that. It was one of those things. It was hard to fall out with big John, and he said he'd never do it again before a game, and he didn't – not to my knowledge anyway.

Styles of Management

I sometimes think about what I would tell myself if I were to go back in time and speak to myself at the start of my journey as a manager. I think the art of management is still very much the same. It is about managing people, as Pep Guardiola says all the time, and as Sir Alex Ferguson, Matt Busby, Brian Clough – all the greats – used to say. As a manager I always tried to think about how I liked being treated as a player and what got the best out of me. Nobody likes criticism, but as a player I felt that if the criticism was levelled at me for a reason, and I deserved it, I could take it. That is very different from ranting and raving and being negative all the time. As a consequence, if I was praised I knew it was genuine and I took it to heart. I tried to manage in a similar way. Brian Clough was very influential in my way of management in that sense, although I didn't necessarily agree with everything he did. For one, he wasn't one for lots of praise, and was really quite harsh sometimes. You do need to criticise players now and again, but I was also keen to praise them when they did well. It is a lot more enjoyable to praise people than criticise them. I think maybe even my approach would seem old fashioned these days because I was very firm with players when I didn't think they were following instructions or pulling their weight. I did find it difficult at Nottingham Forest, where I managed for only 19 games in 2019. I only had one week of pre-season and it was hard to change the players' mentality. I felt as if they were so used to losing football matches that it didn't particularly matter to them. I wanted to change that, and I like to think I would have been able to do so given a bit more time, but it wasn't to be.

Over the last ten years or so there has been that shift in the balance of power at a football club, as discussed elsewhere. Managers have less power, players and agents have more. Another notable change has seen the big rise in the importance of the CEO and the director of football. I never worked under a director of football but now practically every top team has one. The role is supposed to be a conduit between the manager and the chairman, but I think it can lead to a vacuum of responsibility. Sporting directors will get players in, but if those signings do not perform it is the manager who gets the blame. If you're going into a club and there is already a sporting director in place, you'll have to fight your corner over transfers and ways of going about your job, because you don't want players and procedures foisted on you if you're a manager worth your salt. If the results don't go your way, it's you who will get the sack, probably long before the sporting director does. I don't mind the CEO overseeing the business side of things, which a football manager is likely to have less knowledge of. The commercial aspect is far more important now – getting sponsorship deals, things like that – but if the CEO is also interfering in footballing matters you can find yourself in trouble. I really felt that at Sunderland.

Manchester United in recent years have seemed messy in that respect: too many people interfering and no real accountability. There are so many backroom staff now, it's hard to imagine what they all do. If that TV money disappeared, a lot of jobs would disappear as well, although there is no sign of that happening any time soon. Managers like Brian Clough, or more recently Sir Alex Ferguson, were the ultimate source of authority at their clubs. Now players can go over your head as a manager, and things can happen that you are completely unaware of. Agents sometimes don't want to deal directly with managers any more.

It was only rarely that I genuinely fell out with players. There were a couple I did fall out with, but I tended to fall back in with them again. I could lose my temper, there's no question about that, but I would not want to properly fall out with anyone unless something had really gone beyond the pale. Emotions run high in football, especially when you lose, and cross words can be spoken, but it is rare that something casts a shadow for a long period of time. I don't mind saying I was an argumentative manager. I didn't mind taking players on verbally and was sometimes pretty aggressive in the dressing room. I think I was short and sharp and to the point. As I've said, players can't take in loads of information – they will remember the emotion of what you say rather than any detailed instructions. Brian Clough's message was always brief. If you weren't doing your job he would let you know about it. That was very important. If we won a game, though, even if we'd been hanging on at the end . . . winning a match was the most important thing. You can rectify things about the performance during the course of the next week but it is far easier to do that when you've won a game rather than trying to put things right when you've lost. I tended to go overboard in my praise of players, as I may have been too heavy-handed in my moments of criticism. The idea behind the extravagant praise was that criticism of that particular player could be accepted more readily when surely it would fall on him in future games.

Of course, as a manager your aim is to have your players in the best possible frame of mind to play – your job depends on their performances, don't forget.

If relaxation is something you feel benefits your squad – Brian Clough was a big believer in having his team take some down time before big games, and it worked for him – then do so, as long as you convey very positively to the players that this type of preparation will pay dividends.

Relaxation is one thing. Mischief making is an entirely different subject, although frankly I tended to forgive those lovable rascals who came up big in match days much more easily than those rogues who didn't!

Managing the Dressing Room

One of the most difficult things in a dressing room is keeping everyone happy. Although you want lots of say and control as a manager, you have to delegate a bit to the players and give them some responsibility so they don't feel like schoolchildren. Players generally run their own system of fines for lateness and whatever else.

The role of the captain is important, although maybe not so much as in other sports, like cricket. I only captained a side a few times at club level; John McGovern was our longstanding captain at Forest. I was captain of Northern Ireland, though, which I really enjoyed. Captaining Northern Ireland is almost a role beyond football, especially during the Troubles when there was a lot of responsibility on me as a Catholic. It was an honour to captain my country at the Home Championships, a competition involving Northern Ireland, England, Wales and Scotland which no longer exists. Most significantly, I was Northern Ireland captain at the World Cup in Spain in 1982, of course. As I got a bit older I grew a stronger voice, and started to speak up more and more in the dressing room, both at international level, where I was expected to as captain, and for my club, where I became an experienced voice in the squad. As a manager I had various captains. In my seasons at Leicester City I had Steve Walsh as captain for most of the time. Paul Lambert was my captain at Celtic; he could dish it out verbally, and led by example too. Gareth Barry was a good captain for me at Villa – he was one that led by example rather than being very loud. I think it is a manager's role to give responsibility to a captain, and then hopefully the captain feels stronger for it.

As a manager, you are constantly trying to gauge your players' personalities and attitudes, as well as their ability and fitness. I occasionally came across some players who didn't seem too worried about whether they played or didn't play, especially in my later years. It's a minority, but there are certainly players who feign disappointment when they're not in the side but are ultimately not that bothered, and that attitude can be contagious. The best way to keep a dressing room happy is by winning matches, because then you have a positive attitude and the dissenters have no voice. If you start to lose games, you get an atmosphere of disenchantment from the players who have played in the game, plus you will get one or two players giving the impression that the reason for the defeat is that they were not playing. The important thing is not to let the losing run go on for too long. Overall, if you feel as if you're in control of the dressing room, it's OK.

One of the reasons it might feel harder to manage players in the 2020s than in the 1970s is because there has been a gradual shift in attitudes. Sir Alex Ferguson says that his style of management started to change over the course of his career in order to deal with today's players, who have a different outlook on things and find it harder to take criticism. It's all right when you're him, and have lots of big trophies behind you, but managers with lesser reputations have to adapt because players react differently now to how they would have 15 or 20 years ago. When I was a player I felt like I was part of the Nottingham community as well as a Forest player, and while I earned good money, it wasn't at today's level – there was a degree of relatability there. Unquestionably, there is a far bigger distance between players and fans today, and that affects the role of the manager.

When I look back on my time as a manager, some moments stick out. Funnily enough, winning the FA Trophy with Wycombe Wanderers in 1991 was a huge moment for me, even though it was on a tiny stage compared to what would come later. It showed I was making a decent fist of management, and lifting the FA Trophy was what the chairman had always wanted to do. Then we won promotion two years later, of course, the same season as winning the FA Trophy again. This period was the start of a happy three decades as a football manager.

The Wycombe trophies were especially meaningful because my children were old enough by that point to see them and understand it, so those were lovely little memories. Then with Leicester City, there were more trophies. But Steve Walford, who was my coach, once said to me that for all the things that we did at Leicester City – winning two League Cups and finishing in the top ten in four consecutive years – the biggest moment was actually getting promotion to the Premier League, which we did by beating Crystal Palace in the play-off final. That was huge because it is hard to imagine the later magical memories without that one. If we hadn't gone up then I would have been under pressure immediately – lose the final, then the first two matches of the next season, and you're in trouble – because I hadn't won all the Leicester City fans over by that point.

Football memories are shaped by the calendar. Winning European Cups as a player was particularly magical because they were the last games of the season, so you could go out all night – which we did in Madrid in 1980 – and have the time of your life, really, then bask in the glory over the summer. It's the same with winning the play-off final. The emotions are inevitably a bit different when you win the League Cup because the final is usually in late February or early March, so you're right in the thick of the season and don't have a lot of time to enjoy it. It was still amazing though. We won the League Cup in my first full year at Leicester City, our first in the Premier League, which had been a real battle. We didn't have a great start and right up until the last few games of the season it felt as though relegation was a possibility, although remarkably we finished ninth in the end. I think the League Cup really helped. It had been a tough old year, but winning the cup gave us the impetus to carry on.

The lowest low for me was the first time I got sacked in my career, at Sunderland in 2013, after I had been there just over a year. Sunderland were my team as a boy, so having the opportunity to manage them was a huge experience, and it ended on a sour note.

I spoke at a League Managers' Association seminar a while back with younger coaches coming into the game. A lot of them were asking me about the secrets of coaching, what my top tips would be. What I said was that they would all have their own individual personalities, and should put those into practice. 'Your personality should pervade things and you should, in some manner, even if you're a quiet manager, get the players to listen to you.' I tried to look into the minds of the players to see how they could cope with it all. I concluded: 'It's up to you to be able to get players to listen to you. But the best way to do it, of course, is to win football matches. I keep coming back to this, but sometimes the way we talk about football gets away from this basic point: you just have to win. People will follow you if you're winning, because what you're saying to them is ringing true, and any dissent in the dressing room will be quieter. You just have to win.'

10

MEDIA

Everyone has bad days at work, but there are very few careers where you might wake up one morning and the front page of every newspaper says you're completely useless and should be sacked. Perhaps prime minister is one. Football manager is another. In one sense football managers and players rely on the media — if it wasn't there, nobody outside the stadium would know what was going on. On the other hand, it can all be quite overwhelming. The media demands on players and managers have increased hugely in recent years. When I was starting out I barely spoke to the media at all. I cannot recall too many media interviews that I did in my early playing days. Perhaps a few extra when I became captain of Northern Ireland. I assume local radio and the written press would have attempted to do some midweek stories but then again our mercurial manager, Brian Clough would have been in the limelight anyway. So perhaps we Nottingham Forest players had a relatively easy life in terms of press interviews, even at the height of our powers.

Nowadays there is an obligation on managers to speak to the media after every game. Fines may well follow if they decide not to do post-match interviews. Broadcasters have paid lots of money for the access rights. I'm afraid saying something like, 'I'm not really up to it' doesn't go down that well when big money has been spent on finding out what went right and, probably more interestingly, what went wrong in the match just played.

I don't want to make out that media commitment is a terribly arduous thing to do. Managers don't mind doing interviews as a rule. It's good to get your message out there. But the sheer number of them can feel excessive, and it seems to only increase. I saw this changing in my time at Aston Villa between 2006 and 2010. The minute the game is over, you would do a quick interview for Sky, then go into the big media room and do your press conference with a room full of journalists, followed by an interview for BBC Radio 5 Live, and then a piece for the local radio stations, speaking to different people each time. There are often foreign broadcasters in the mix as well now. It can be very tiring, and there are a million other priorities after a big game.

You end up saying the same thing each time, and in your own mind you think, 'I just said that 15 minutes ago.' You try to change it a little bit, but in an attempt to do that you might put an emphasis on something that you didn't really mean to, and it can often end up in the news in ways you might not always see coming. The stakes are high in any interview for a manager. Reporters are desperate for a new line, and you can say one slightly wrong thing, or even just word something quite casually, and it turns into a story that can run for days. There is just so much media now. You do a press conference the day before each game, so you would do one on Friday for a Saturday, and Tuesday for Wednesday. It means if you're playing midweek and at the weekend it's almost every day that you're having to speak to the media – or it certainly feels like it. And there are many opportunities to slip up. On more than one occasion, I let off some steam at either pre- or post-match interviews. Not only did I instantly regret this, but I also found myself up in the FA Courts in order for the error of my ways to be pointed out.

In my early days as a manager at Wycombe I didn't have a huge amount of media scrutiny compared to what came later. I spent most of my time in England managing teams that were trying to punch above their weight a bit – Wycombe in the Football League, and then Leicester and Villa in the Premier League where the focus was a lot greater. I often said things I shouldn't have because I genuinely felt that referees didn't give my teams things they might have given to Manchester United. Between 1993 and 2004 the away side was given only three penalties in the league at Old Trafford, and they were all missed! If you're a referee, and you want some kind words said to you by a manager, you might as well have those kind words said by Sir Alex Ferguson because he was such a respected figure. They do not want to be going home, having a late meal before *Match of the Day* comes on, and Ferguson is saying, 'I thought the referee was terrible.' Whereas if you upset Aston Villa or Leicester City there is less of a backlash.

MEDIA

The last decade has seen the decline in print media. You might think the days of print newspapers having a huge audience are ancient history, but it was the case really not that long ago. Scotland's *Daily Record* is based in Glasgow, and a huge part of what sells papers is news about Celtic and Rangers. In 2005, when I left Celtic, its daily circulation was 450,000. Two decades later it was just 50,000. That is a huge shift in the Scottish media landscape. So much 'news' has moved online now, not necessarily to respectable outlets where journalists check their facts. People are looking for instant news and have got out of the habit of paying for it, so the quality is often low. Not that it was always brilliant from the established newspapers. In my time in Glasgow, Celtic were so big everyone wanted a new story all the time, and sometimes someone would pick up on a word that I'd said and twist the meaning of it. Quite regularly I would say something in a light-hearted way and see it written up as serious commentary. There were about 15 pages given over to sport in the *Daily Record* in Scotland, with plenty more in the *Sun* and other papers, and often football was on the front page as well. After a while you realise that it's all just a bit of a game. Sometimes I took the media side of things a bit too seriously, and felt as if I was taking the moral high ground. I wish I hadn't done so at times, even if I knew a story was fanciful at best. In my latter stages I took it less seriously but there were times when things got exaggerated and I got a bit annoyed. There were other times when things were printed which were categorically untrue. I took out a few legal cases and won a few when the media printed things that were libellous. There was one, during my stay at Celtic, that alleged a conflict of interest with an agent. It was totally made up, and I won damages. Even if you win the case it's not great because the story is still out there.

Punditry

I am still involved in the media these days, but on the other side of things as a pundit. I enjoy the analysis side of football. A lot of pundits are fairly recent ex-players who have not managed, so I can hopefully provide a different viewpoint there. Even over the course of the few years I've been doing punditry there is now just so much more of it out there, so many more games on TV, and often more expected of you as a pundit. I make sure to do my homework. I watch an awful lot of football from all over the world. I will always prepare some thoughts on the two managers and what they might be going through at the time: the pressures, the relationships with the players and the people higher up, the transfer situation, where they might be looking to strengthen in the next window. That's what I try to focus on as it's where I think I can add insight. As well as working for UK broadcasters I've also worked for Mola TV based in Indonesia, which I enjoyed. In the 2023–24 season I covered all of Como's games in the Italian second division, which was a bit different but I enjoyed discovering a new level of football. It was all done out of an office in London, but I got to know the Como players inside out from watching them so often. They got promoted which meant the company lost the rights. I wanted them to do well, but perhaps now in hindsight I shouldn't have wanted them to get promoted! In the 2022 World Cup I did punditry for Astro TV, a Malaysian broadcaster, not from Qatar where the World Cup was being held, but in a studio in Kuala Lumpur. The Malaysians are lovely people to work for. I've worked for all the big UK broadcasters, as well as Sky, Amazon and TNT. They often ask me to work on games involving my former clubs, as well as others too. I don't offer myself around that much. If they ask me, I'll probably do it if I'm able to, but if they don't, it doesn't bother me – I have plenty going on elsewhere. I always enjoy it when I'm there, although the jobs do seem to be getting longer and longer. Sometimes they want you to be on TV for an hour and a half before the game starts, which feels like a very long time, believe me. The host and the team are always very professional, and they have video packages to break things up, but it's a lot of time to fill – you really do need to do your homework.

Modern punditry began in the 1970s. I don't remember there being punditry for the 1966 World Cup – they just showed the game in those days. Things all changed shortly after that. Jimmy Hill was the main voice at ITV, but there was Pat Crerand and Derek Dougan too. They set a pretty high standard and were clearly having a great time in the studio, and it all became a big thing. People tuned in to the studio chat as much as they did to the games. Punditry grew, and I feel lucky to have been involved in so much of it over the years. One good thing about doing it is you get to meet some very interesting people, like, as I mentioned, Johan Cruyff during Euro 2000 on the BBC. I have got to meet great players from more recent generations as well. There's a clip on YouTube that still sometimes does the rounds. In 2014 at the World Cup in Brazil I was a studio guest alongside Patrick Vieira and Fabio Cannavaro – two great players who had won the World Cup for France and Italy respectively. The host, Adrian Chiles, was trying to make a little joke at my expense and I had to remind him that despite the fact we were in the company of two World Cup winners, when it comes to the Champions League – or European Cup – I'd won it twice. I happened to know that those two never had. A lot of people talk to me about that clip! I was out two nights later with Cannavaro and the ITV team; it was a lot of fun out there.

A new thing recently is that broadcasters often want pundits pitch-side rather than in a warm studio. I can see why, because it looks nice on TV, and it's good when you can grab a player or manager for a quick interview at the end of the game. It can get very cold out there though. I prefer to be in a warm studio. How it works is that just before the game kicks off you rush into a trailer in the car park to watch the game on a monitor with a set of headphones on, and then rush back to do the on-screen analysis at half-time. To be there on time you often have to leave the trailer a bit before the half-time whistle, so you end up missing the last few minutes of the half, during which you're praying not much happens. As soon as the half-time whistle blows you run on to the pitch, they show some adverts, and you're on. You could have missed two goals, and be ready with your analysis of 43 minutes in which nothing much happened.

I always enjoy chatting to current managers, in formal media situations as well as more casually. In February 2025 I went up to Glasgow to do a package with Amazon Prime which included interviewing Brendan Rodgers, one of my successors as Celtic manager, who has won a lot of trophies there. The club had finished the new training ground, Lennoxtown, in 2007 which was after I had left. I went to view the site when it was just a load of fields, but it was the first time I had been there since it was complete. Brendan was very amenable.

It can be tricky as a pundit to criticise managers, because you know what it's like to be in their shoes, and often you might know them personally too. As the chairman of the League Managers' Association, my views need to be balanced and any criticism constructive. But I do always say that managers know what they're stepping into. You've got to win. If you don't win football matches, nothing is going to save you – it doesn't really matter what else you do or say. I don't mind being critical of someone I know and like as a person, though, in terms of saying that they've got to win. There's a decent chance that if they keep winning football matches they'll stay in the job, and if you win enough, you might end up winning a trophy, and that gives you a lot of power. Managers know all this and it's nothing personal. For your own credibility as a pundit, you've got to criticise sometimes – nobody wants to listen to a former manager just defending other managers the whole time, especially when it's clear things are going badly. I do think the great pundit should be above personal relationships.

I find that a lot of pundits, particularly those who have played the game at a decent level but have never managed, sometimes ascribe too much power and influence to the manager. Sometimes a defeat is a manager's fault – perhaps he's tried something tactically that hasn't worked, or left out a good player or put in someone who wasn't fully fit. But most of the time the team with the better players will win, and a game will hinge on a moment of skill or perhaps a mistake. The manager can have an impact during the game, certainly, but it is a small one. Pundits frequently say that if a team has conceded a goal it is because a manager has got his tactics wrong, but it's often not as clear as that. If a team's shape is wrong that could be down to a player error, someone standing out of position, or not getting back quick enough. Brian Clough was very astute at all that despite not having the benefit of as many cameras and replays. If you had conceded but had been trying something positive at the other end, he would recognise that.

Pundits can be wrong about a player being at fault as well. You might see a short clip on social media and say the team conceded a goal because one particular player was out of position. But if you scroll back 15 seconds before that, the same player might have made a good run down the field, lost the ball trying to do the right thing, and had to travel 60 yards to get back into this position – so somebody else should be covering for him. You have to leave spaces sometimes in football if you're going to attack and score goals; you can't have every player just sitting back and inviting pressure. That is especially true if you're behind in a game – you need to commit players forward, which obviously carries the risk of leaving holes and conceding another, but that is better than just accepting your fate. The reasons things happen in a football match are often more complicated than they look. Sometimes when you concede a goal it's not because of an identifiable coaching error or individual mistake, it's just part of football: even the best teams concede goals; maybe it was a particularly brilliant shot, or bit of skill from an opposing player. Another utterance you often hear is that a manager should have made substitutions at a particular time, that his substitutes came on too late. If a team loses a game, that is often the first thing people say. I rarely agree with that. It's not to say substitutions don't matter – of course they do – but they are rarely the main reason why you win or lose a game of football.

Football can be hard to analyse because a huge part of it is luck – and it's a low-scoring game where one individual mistake or fortunate bounce of the ball is the difference between triumph or disaster. If I've said it once, I've said it a thousand times: the winning of the game is the most important thing. However you've won that game that day, whether it was in the lap of the gods or whether you've been brilliant . . . winning is the main thing. Eventually, if you're winning a number of matches by fluke, that will catch up with you and you will start to lose. But if you've played badly on the day and won the game, you can rectify that during the week. It's crazy because there can only be so many winners in a season. Only one team can win the Premier League, and the various cups. If you finish runners-up or in the semi-finals, who remembers? The UEFA Cup final in 2003 is remembered by Celtic fans as an unbelievable experience in Seville. There were 75,000 fans in the city, without one arrest. That's amazing, it's great they had such a good time, and the journey was fantastic. But we lost. It would have been Celtic's first major European trophy since Jock Stein in 1967. It would have been lovely, but we lost. If I were to go back and change one thing, it would absolutely be that.

Aside from punditry, I only briefly tried my hand at commentary – and got into a lot of trouble for it. It was when I was a player. There was a barrister in Nottingham called Graham Richards, who was also a football commentator. He knew I had an interest in law and crime. One evening he asked me if I would do co-commentary for a midweek game – not a Forest one – and I said yes without thinking. I should have asked my manager Brian Clough, who never liked Graham. The following morning I went into training and Clough brought me aside. He said, 'I heard your dulcet tones last night. Here's your fine.' I asked why he was fining me, and he said, 'You never asked. I probably wouldn't have allowed you to do it anyway. But I'm fining you.' He was absolutely right to do so. With Clough, for anything like that, you'd first have to ask permission.

As it happens I've got another story about the commentator Graham Richards. He had been commentating for Radio Nottingham and then he moved to Radio Derby. It was no secret that he was a big Derby fan, but I maintained a friendship with him nevertheless. It was 1979 and Forest were playing Derby away at the Baseball Ground, the predecessor to the Pride Park stadium that replaced it in 1997. As a former Derby manager, keenly aware of the East Midlands rivalry between the clubs, Clough really did not want to lose that game. We were reigning European champions, but we got hammered 4–1.

Clough knew Graham Richards was friendly with me because of that commentary incident a couple of seasons earlier. Right by the dressing rooms in the Baseball Ground was a little room that Radio Derby would use for interviews. It was only about ten minutes after the game had ended and Clough was in the middle of dressing us down after a poor performance when there was a knock at the door. It was Graham Richards. He was gesturing to me, asking me to come on his programme. Clough looked around, and asked Richards what he wanted. 'I'll go on your programme,' he said, to Richards' surprise.

Richards then ran down the corridor to tell his colleagues to warn the radio station that Brian Clough was soon coming to them live. For some reason, Richards always used to come to the games with these two mates of his. I don't recall their names – let's call them Tom and Fred. Wherever he went, Tom and Fred would be there too, and they were sitting in the radio room with Richards, waiting for Clough. Brian Clough walked in, sat down, and asked Richards who the friends were.

'These are my two friends,' he said.

'What are their names?' Clough asked.

Clough looked Tom in the eye, shook his hand, held eye contact and said, 'F**k off.' He then did the same to Fred. He shook his hand as if he was going to be nice and then said, 'F**k off.' They left.

Then the interview began, and Clough was asked about the chastening performance at the hands of Derby County.

'I couldn't care less, Graham. What the fans want to know is: who do you support?' Whatever question Clough was asked, he brought it back to that, deflecting any questions about the game. Then he cleared out of the room without having answered any questions about the match. He arrived back in the dressing room, came up to me, and said, 'Tell your mate he's the worst f**king commentator that's ever f**king lived.'

The Language of Football

One thing that frustrates me about modern punditry is that it feels like you have to speak about football in a certain way, which has all moved quite far from my own understanding of the game. For example: 'assists'. The modern media is obsessed with assists. That wasn't a common concept in my days as a player. An 'assist' is just the last player to touch the ball before the goalscorer. Of course, sometimes a goal is the result of a brilliant cross or pass, but I think we put far too much emphasis on assists nowadays, adding them together with goals to accrue 'goal contributions', which is ridiculous. You can be given an assist if you've barely played any role in a goal. There is a famous one, Tottenham against Inter Milan, where Peter Crouch, next to his own penalty area, gave the ball to Gareth Bale and then Bale ran down the entire pitch and scored, but Crouch was credited with an 'assist'. Scoring a goal is a lot harder than getting an assist. A manager like Brian Clough would recognise the real creator of a goal by telling them so in the dressing room, and it wouldn't necessarily be the player who got the 'assist'. He might praise a defensive player who stopped an attacking move, then played the ball to someone deep in our own half, leading to a goal being scored maybe 40 or 50 seconds later. He would never use the word 'assist', but he would say, 'You got us that because you stopped the move in the first place, then the ball ends up in the opposition net.' He would come into the dressing room at half-time and make such observations – which were good because they made you focus on what matters, not just the final pass.

What's funny about all this is that when we talk about the great modern players, we always talk about how many goals and assists they rack up each season, but in my playing days assists were just never mentioned. When it comes to my playing career the goals are all there in the history books, and, as I said, a lot of them were scored at the back post from a John Robertson cross.

As for assists, I have no idea. They simply weren't recorded, and very few of those games are available on video. I definitely got a lot of assists but the number literally doesn't exist, and there will be no way of ever knowing.

I don't mind too much, though. The way I see it, for a winger an assist is just another word for doing your job. It wasn't until the early 2000s that assists were measured in the Premier League. Someone had to go back to 1992 and watch all the old games to count them up, so there are complete statistics going back that far, but further back we have no idea, and never will. John Robertson must have got a ridiculous number of assists. He was, of course, on the opposite wing to me at Forest, and his goalscoring was pretty decent too – but his assists were off the scale. He made so many goals for us.

Along with assists, the other big statistic that comes up a lot in punditry these days is 'expected goals'. I think this is total nonsense. You've got to remember what the game is about: winning football matches, and that means scoring goals, not recording the expectation of them. 'Expected goals' have only come about in the last few years. I think it's a clueless development. I think some people just use these words to try to sound clever. That is one of my issues with doing punditry now – the language keeps evolving, but I don't think it makes people understand the game better; I think it makes it more confusing. When it comes to football discussions today I think there is far too much jargon employed. I find it difficult, not because I don't like change but simply because use of the terminology seems excessive. It's not that people necessarily believe in what they're saying, it's because they feel as if they have to factor it in. They want to be really clever in the sense of telling you something that you didn't know, but a lot of it is rubbish. I have always felt football is a simple game, even if it doesn't make me sound clever saying that.

Meeting Fans

One of the reasons managers care about the media is that it influences how fans think of them. Despite the fierce rivalries some of my teams have featured in, my interactions with football fans outside of work have almost always been pleasant. I always enjoyed meeting fans out and about. Although people might shout horrible things in a football stadium, I found it was actually very rare that things turned nasty in real life. Even after five years in Glasgow, where you might think meeting Rangers fans would be an issue, I honestly can count on the fingers of one hand the number of times I was verbally abused, or people gave me hassle when I was out with my family. We would be sensible about where we went, of course. If the whole team was out together to celebrate a big victory, we would generally book an entire restaurant, not go somewhere where there would be fans milling around. But for smaller events it was never really an issue. On a Saturday night, if we'd won a game, I might go with my coaches John Robertson and Steve Walford and their families to grab a bite to eat. You would have people come up to your table, of course. Celtic fans would come over to you and would want to take photographs and say, 'Well done.' The Rangers fans generally just left you alone.

I remember one occasion, when we lost to Rangers in the semi-final of the League Cup at Hampden, I got home quite late because it was an evening kick-off, and somebody had put a big Union Jack in my garden. I took it more as a bit of fun than anything else. A few years later, though, Celtic manager Neil Lennon received some really horrible threats, so I was lucky that never happened to me. That didn't mean that when you went to Ibrox you didn't get slated, of course, but it is different when you're on the job and there are security and police around; I never worried about my own safety there, or while on the touchline in any other stadium. Some of the nastier stuff I experienced was as a player. I was playing for Northern Ireland as a Catholic in a team that was roughly half Catholic, half Protestant – but most of the fans were Protestants. Sometimes I would get stick from my own fans. When the manager Billy Bingham made me captain of the team it didn't go down too well. I was the first Catholic captain of Northern Ireland, and there was some backlash. He did say it would all blow over if we started to win some football matches, which we did. We qualified for Spain in 1982, and nobody was too bothered about who was Catholic or Protestant while we were winning games at the World Cup. In my earlier days there were some hairy moments, though. My brothers would be in the stands and would be listening to the people in the crowd hurling abuse at me, a player for their own team.

Modern Media

When it comes to football in the media, portraying the game in fiction is easier said than done. One film I really enjoyed is *Mike Bassett: England Manager*, starring Ricky Tomlinson. He tells everyone to 'f**k off' all the time, which is exactly what you want to say to people when you're a manager. It is a bit over the top, but I really enjoyed it. Another good film is *The Damned United*, based on a book by David Peace, about Brian Clough's brief reign at Leeds United. Not so long ago in an airport I bumped into Michael Sheen, the actor who played Clough in the film. I told him he absolutely captured the essence of the man. We had a nice chat. The film was excellent, although there were some serious inaccuracies in it and the production company ended up getting sued. One incident concerned Dave Mackay, who had been a great player, hard as nails and as courageous as they come. The film made it look like Mackay had betrayed Brian Clough by replacing him as Derby manager. They got that horribly wrong. Mackay sued and won. Mackay wasn't a traitor, he was coming in as a manager at Derby because Brian Clough was leaving. The film's portrayal was inaccurate. Johnny Giles, another great player, also sued successfully because the film portrayed him as a scheming character. There were lots of smaller inaccuracies too – getting a scoreline wrong, and things like that. It was a great film, though, with fantastic acting – I'll give them that. It is hard to make the actual game of football look realistic in films and TV, but they did a really good job, filming at Chesterfield's old Saltergate ground, which is quite old fashioned, so it looked the part. The actor Stephen Graham, who is now a massive star, did a really good job of playing Billy Bremner at Leeds.

I had little to do with the internet in my time in management. In my later years some of my staff or players might have been in WhatsApp groups, but I wouldn't have been in them. I certainly was never on social media, which only became a big thing towards the end of my career when I was managing Ireland. The only time I became aware of it was when my daughters would see some criticism and would inadvertently mention it to me, but I would never seek it out myself. Such content often came from people who hadn't been at the game or even watched it, so I didn't care too much what they thought. But there is no doubt that it is having a big impact on the game now.

I think some players don't have the same respect for their club and their manager now, and feel like they are free to say whatever they want on social media. When Marcus Rashford left Manchester United to go to Aston Villa on loan in January 2025, Jadon Sancho, who was on loan at Chelsea from United at the time, posted 'freedom' on Instagram under Rashford's post.

There's nothing more irritating for a manager to hear than that. There were stories about Jadon Sancho at Manchester United being regularly late for training. You get paid all that money and you can't get out of bed? I don't understand it. It's as if to say it was somebody else's fault that he didn't do well. Players – and I would include myself in my playing days in this – are not very good at looking at themselves when thinking about why they might be falling short. As a manager you feel the pressure of bad results, maybe too much so, but I think some players don't feel that pressure enough despite earning huge sums and putting in poor performances.

I'm not saying everything was better in my day. Perhaps it would have been good if players had had a little more power back then, and the ability to get their message across in the media, which social media has brought in. But there has been a rise in complacency, sensitivity and just not caring enough. Back then, every Saturday that you missed, either through being left out of a team or through injury, was a Saturday you felt you weren't going to get back again. It felt really important to play, not just for me but for the whole Nottingham Forest team. We wanted to play, and it was such a disappointment not to. Lots of players now seem happy not to play, perhaps picking up an injury and spending a long time recovering, even when you're sure they're fine.

As a manager you are always in the media spotlight and it can be exhausting. It sometimes feels like success is shared but failure sits heavily on the manager's shoulders. I'm not complaining – as I've said, it's what managers sign up for – but it is difficult, and why I think management is not for everyone. There is respite when you win a couple of games, but then you're back in the limelight again when things are not going so well. Your job is constantly being talked about. The media spotlight does affect you – of course it does – and your family as well. Understandably, it can affect your personal life. It's not so much the hours, working every weekend and being really busy all the time. You know that's part of the job, and it's an immense privilege. But some of the criticism can get to you if results aren't going well, especially if you think people are being unfair or saying things that aren't true. You don't want to be seen as a failure in your own home.

It was particularly intense at Celtic, where the whole city is obsessed and the rivalry is so fierce. You want to insulate your family from anything nasty. When I started at Celtic my elder daughter had gone away to university but my younger one was still at school, and we moved her to a school closer to us for her A-levels. She railed against it at first. I remember her room had a glass roof, and she would spend nights up there in the cold; it was her protest, a bit like the prisoners of Strangeways in Manchester. We would call her and she just wouldn't come down. Over time though she grew to love it, and now her three best pals are from the school in Scotland. Luckily things went pretty well there on the football pitch. We won a domestic treble in my first season, which hopefully made the adjustment easier for my family.

I think managers got a bit less scrutiny and a bit more time in my playing days, and that was probably a good thing. The media is a 24-hour machine now, and people are constantly looking to fill space on TV and radio stations and on social media. Once the weekend fixtures are finished, they need stories to fill airtime, and 'manager on the brink' is always a good story. If, early in my career, you had a terrible result there might have been some bad headlines the next day, maybe a column or two, but it felt like there was eventually an end to it. But now the post-match frenzy can roll on for days online, especially if there's an international break and everyone's looking for things to fill space with.

The pressure was different back then, although, of course, it could still be fierce – just look at Brian Clough's time at Leeds United, where he only lasted 44 days. Even so, if you had a reputation, a bad run felt less apocalyptic. Clough started his Forest career with two wins but after that we went on a very long run without a victory. Only Brian Clough could have survived that, not least because he had already proved himself at Derby. In the modern game he might have been hounded out. With Sir Alex Ferguson, too, fans wanted him to go in 1989, but he clung on and that turned out OK. More recently, Mikel Arteta had a fairly poor first season with Arsenal before a big improvement. But, generally, it feels like managers get less time now, and part of that must be because the media frenzy is so much more relentless. Managers' decisions are picked over for days on end, but, as we've seen, there are so many factors that go into whether you win or lose a football match. The media situation is just so intense now. It might be good for the football-obsessed public, so it is hard to say if it is entirely a bad thing – and it is also probably something that I have benefited from. But I am glad not to be a manager under that intense spotlight any more.

CONCLUSION

I am a dreamer about the game. I love it.

Has football changed for the better? This is the question I have been asking myself while writing this book, thinking of the aspects which stand out as particularly positive or negative. Now, when I look back on the 1970s, one of the first things I think about is those boggy pitches. They were terrible – terrible for the players, the spectators, the referee, everybody. It was a completely different game in the summer to the winter, and not in a good way. Nowadays you can turn on your TV or go to a game in January and you know the players will be able to actually kick the ball. It might seem a trivial thing, but I think better pitches are an unbelievable improvement to the game. Back then, for a good chunk of the year you could not actually play proper football. The change is credit to the ground staff and technology people who make it work.

Another huge improvement is that the fighting in the stands, the hooliganism, racism, and all that awful stuff in the 1970s and 1980s has been hugely cleaned up. A football stadium is a safe place for a family to go these days – a comfortable place to go – and you certainly would not always have been able to say that. There have been massive improvements in the physical fitness of players too, which makes the game more intense and hard-running.

When I think about what has got worse in football, the thing that annoys me the most is the constant diving and feigning injury. I really think it is getting a lot worse. My understanding from the referees I've spoken to is that it's partly attributable to the new rule introduced to stop the game for head injuries, which is sensible, but open to abuse by players. I don't like the level of money in the game either, which increasingly flows to the top. It is getting harder for the normal fan to afford a ticket. Ordinary fans wanting to take children to a game are being priced out of football, which is something I thought would not happen.

In some senses, though, the game really hasn't changed that much. The pitch markings are the same; the rules are almost the same; a lot of the culture of football – what managers say, how players motivate themselves – has changed less than you think. All of which makes me think that while football might change some more over the next 50 years, it might change less than other aspects of the world. If you go back a century, or 150 years, to the very origins of football, it was very different of course, but still instantly recognisable, and has changed far less than other aspects of our lives. Football can be a bit of a constant in that respect, something relatively unchanging in a fast-changing world.

Things will continue to develop; I have no doubt about it. Players will become even fitter than they are now, equipment and stadiums will improve. I think the game will become even more fast-paced, just as the game of the 1970s was quicker than the game of the 1930s. That is all only going in one direction. I think football crowds generally want the same thing: move the ball forward quickly, rather than spending too long passing it around at the back; I think there has been a bit of a backlash to some of the tactics that can make the game a little dull to watch. It really is a simple game, made more complicated by people wanting to feel as if they are inventing something new. For all the tactical innovations and jargon you hear, a goal still very often comes from something simple, like a set-piece, some tricky play by a winger, or a skilful pass to a striker. I am optimistic about the future of football. I don't want to mourn the past, or rail against the changes that have taken place. The game is as popular as it is for a reason.

When I think about how football has changed, I often wonder what would happen if you brought back to life someone from my time in the game, perhaps George Best, Bill Shankly or Brian Clough, or Herbert Chapman long before that. No doubt there would be things they would dislike or find uncomfortable – the passing out from the back, the way the game now caters to the middle classes and is geared towards corporate entertainment rather than a simple pastime that sprung up from working-class communities and factory floors. But after giving it some thought, I think those great men would have a wry smile on their faces, because for all the changes, football is fundamentally what it always has been. It is a simple game, and an almost unimprovable one. It has given me so much happiness and joy in life, and I know it will do the same for so many people, long after I am gone.

ACKNOWLEDGMENTS

Thanks to Joey, whose help in putting the book together was invaluable. In fact, without it, the book wouldn't have been written.

To Oli whose idea it was in the first place and to Matt at Northbank for making it happen.

To Zoe, endlessly enthusiastic and tirelessly supportive, but in need of a good holiday after working with me.

And finally to the Headline team, my family for their support, those who have enriched my playing and managerial career and to all who dedicate themselves to the beautiful game.

RAISING READERS
Books Build Bright Futures

Dear Reader,

We'd love your attention for one more page to tell you about the crisis in children's reading, and what we can all do.

Studies have shown that reading for fun is the **single biggest predictor of a child's future success** – more than family circumstance, parents' educational background or income. It improves academic results, mental health, wealth, communication skills and ambition.

The number of children reading for fun is in rapid decline. Young people have a lot of competition for their time, and a worryingly high number do not have a single book at home.

Our business works extensively with schools, libraries and literacy charities, but here are some ways we can all raise more readers:

- Reading to children for just 10 minutes a day makes a difference
- Don't give up if your children aren't regular readers – there will be books for them!
- Visit bookshops and libraries to get recommendations
- Encourage them to listen to audiobooks
- Support school libraries
- Give books as gifts

Thank you for reading.
www.JoinRaisingReaders.com